Writing and Selling
Your Novel

Writing

and

Selling Your Novel

Jack M. Bickham

WRITER'S DIGEST BOOKS
CINCINNATI, OHIO

Writing and Selling Your Novel. Copyright © 1996 by Jack M. Bickham. Printed and bound in the United States of America. All rights reserved. No part of this book may be reproduced in any form or by any electronic or mechanical means including information storage and retrieval systems without permission in writing from the publisher, except by a reviewer, who may quote brief passages in a review. Published by Writer's Digest Books, an imprint of F&W Publications, Inc., 1507 Dana Avenue, Cincinnati, Ohio 45207. (800) 289-0963. This book is a revised edition of one previously published under the title *Writing Novels That Sell*, published in 1989 by Fireside Books, an imprint of Simon & Schuster, Inc.

This hardcover edition of *Writing and Selling Your Novel* features a "self-jacket" that eliminates the need for a separate dust jacket. It provides sturdy protection for your book while it saves paper, trees and energy.

Other fine Writer's Digest Books are available from your local bookstore or direct from the publisher.

00 99 98 97 96   5 4 3 2 1

Library of Congress Cataloging-in-Publication Data

Bickham, Jack M.
  Writing and selling your novel / Jack M. Bickham.
      p.   cm.
  Rev. ed. of: Writing novels that sell. © 1989.
  Includes bibliographical references and index.
  ISBN 0-89879-788-8 (alk. paper)
  1. Fiction—Authorship. I. Title.
PN3365.B5   1996
808.3—dc20   96-30217
                                                              CIP

Edited by Jack Heffron and Roseann S. Biederman
Cover designed by Brian Roeth
Interior designed by Julie Martin

ABOUT THE AUTHOR

Jack Bickham has published more than eighty novels, including thrillers, mysteries and westerns. Three of his novels have
been made into films, the best known of which is Disney's
The Apple-Dumpling Gang. He has written a number of articles
for *Writer's Digest* magazine and four other books for Writer's
Digest Books: *Scene and Structure, The 38 Most Common Fiction
Writing Mistakes (and How to Avoid Them), Setting,* and *Writing
the Short Story.* For many years he taught creative writing on
the faculty at the University of Oklahoma. He retired several
years ago, but still lives in Norman, Oklahoma.

TABLE OF CONTENTS

Foreword viii

PART ONE
Bedrock Fundamentals...1

One   **THE PROFESSIONAL ATTITUDE**..3

Two   **WORK HABITS AND THE IMAGINATION**.....................19

Three   **THE NATURE OF STORY**...27

Four   **SHOW ME FIRST!**..36

PART TWO
Essential Techniques...41

Five   **VIEWPOINT**..43

Six   **STIMULUS AND RESPONSE**.......................................61

Seven   **GOAL MOTIVATION AND THE STORY QUESTION**..73

Eight   **HOW A STORY STARTS– AND HOW IT ENDS**...83

Nine   **SCENE AND SEQUEL**...93

Ten   **SETTING AND MOOD**...110

Eleven   **HANDLING STORY TIME**..120

Twelve   **CHARACTERS MAKE THE DIFFERENCE**.......................128

Thirteen   **MAKING STORY PEOPLE**

               MORE INTERESTING 147

Fourteen   **DIALOGUE AND NARRATION**..161

PART THREE

Fine Tuning for Sales...173

Fifteen   **BACKSTORY AND HIDDEN STORY** 175

Sixteen   **STORY ARCHITECTURE** 183

Seventeen   **REVISION TECHNIQUES** 194

Eighteen   **GETTING IT SOLD** 201

Nineteen   **FINAL WORDS** 208

               Bibliography 210

               Index...212

FOREWORD

This book represents a complete revision and expansion of an earlier one titled *Writing Novels That Sell*. Several new chapters have been added, and others updated to meet new demands of the commercial marketplace.

The principles of dramaturgy and scene structure at the heart of the earlier book have not changed. You can see them at work in classic novels of the past; you can see them equally well in the latest best-seller at your bookstore. Additional proof that these principles still work can be found in the letters I continue to receive from writers reporting first-novel sales. Therefore the basic assumptions underlying this edition have not changed.

Another thing that has not changed is the fact that you *will* sell your manuscript if it's good enough. Therefore this book, like the earlier one, takes first things first: It aims at making you good enough.

Since publication of the earlier version of this book, however, changes in the publishing scene have made it clear that some new material should be added to keep you up to date and to make sure your manuscript will be as appealing as possible to today's editors. In addition, since that first version I have worked with several hundred more students—and have written some other books on the craft of writing—and flatter myself to think I have learned a bit more myself. Thus, while some of the present volume will be vaguely familiar to readers of the earlier work, much has been altered and, I believe, improved.

I hope all of it will be helpful.

—J.M.B.

PART ONE

Bedrock Fundamentals

Chapter One

The Professional Attitude

Quite possibly there has never been a more difficult time for a new writer to break into the field with a first novel. But that does not mean it is impossible.

If you are an authentic genius, of course, breaking in won't even be difficult. Somehow, by some freak of genetics, you already know everything. There are possibly two or three authentic geniuses every century.

If you're not one of those two or three, however, you need a professional attitude toward your work today more than ever before if you are to break through and get published.

Of course you'll need talent, too. But "talent" is a mysterious quality that can emerge only *after* a professional attitude has been cultivated and fully developed. To put this another way, "talent" is what people say you have after you have worked like hell for years to improve yourself.

The fact that you are reading this book proves you have the first attributes necessary to become "talented": curiosity and the desire to learn.

The other attribute you need to develop is the professional attitude.

What is that, you ask?

It's what made tennis great Billie Jean King wear out several pairs of tennis shoes *every week* when she was young, practicing on the court every day until after dark.

It's what made basketball immortal Bill Russell—already a star—study moves made by other NBA players, then practice them endlessly until they became his own.

It's what made Margaret Mitchell go through countless rewrites of *Gone With the Wind* in order to get everything just right.

Great practitioners in any field make it look easy, so bystanders murmur in awe about talent. What the bystander never sees is the agony of effort, study and practice that made the final performance appear effortless—the fruits of professional attitude. So you must, first and foremost, think and work like a professional, with the attitude of a professional.

There are many things involved.

SERIOUSNESS OF PURPOSE

Good professional writing is not a hobby, a time-filler or a lark. It isn't "an easy way to make money in your spare time."

It isn't part-time, strictly speaking, because the professional writer's head is in his work even when his body isn't at the word processor. And the professional knows that in order to succeed he must have regular work hours, a regular workplace and production quotas he *will* meet, even if other important tasks don't get done that day.

It's far too easy to kid yourself about your seriousness of purpose. Once I went a few weeks between book projects. When I tried to return to the desk, I found I "didn't have time." Days passed. Every day, other vital tasks intervened, making it impossible for me to write.

Scared that I might be through as a writer, I made a list of all the things I needed to do the next day. The list looked something like this:

Work at newspaper nine hours
Mow lawn
Spend time with the kids
Answer three letters
Wash car
Watch TV news
Eat
Read evening paper
Help with supper dishes
Write!

I was dismayed until I got a brilliant idea. I turned the list upside down, got up at 5 A.M. and wrote *first*. This got me right back into the swing of things.

It seems so obvious and fundamental. But I have had so

many students who failed this first test of professionalism. They talked endlessly, and even enthusiastically, about how they were going to write just as soon as they had time, or just as soon as they felt better, or just as soon as their lives became less complicated. But they never did get going, some of them; they just kept on kidding themselves and never got anything done.

So please indulge me; let me restate the point. You *will* write if you're professional. Now. Furthermore, to assure professional production, you will set a time and a place, and a page quota, for your work.

Not, please, a time quota. If you say, "I'm going to sit at the desk two hours a day," that's exactly what you'll do—sit. But if you promise yourself that you're going to write five pages a day (or ten!), and stick with that decision, then you won't just sit there very long. You'll get productive in self-defense. The imagination, after all, can be viewed as just another muscle. All muscles are lazy. They have to be worked regularly and hard in order to function at maximum efficiency, and without undue pain.

If you allow yourself to sit idle at the processor for a few hours every day, and then delude yourself that you are meeting a professional-type schedule, your imagination will always fail you. Only when you make it clear to your own imagination that you *will* sit there until pages are produced—however long that may take—only then will the imagination start producing in order to prevent necrosis of the buns.

And the more often you force this kind of work on your imagination, the more readily will it get on with the task.

No professional ever was easy on herself. There are always excuses. You have to jettison all of them and get to work.

DEDICATION TO THE CRAFT
Writing is a craft with learned skills. There is nothing very mysterious about a lot of it. You must, to be professional, respect craftsmanship and give up mystical baloney about "inspiration" and other stuff that doesn't exist except in the fevered imagination of a few deluded English teachers.

To be professional, you must not only respect craftsmanship, but work all your life to identify and learn more of the skills involved in this craft of ours. It doesn't matter how tired you get, or how discouraged. If you aren't selling yet, it's because you haven't learned enough technique. You have to be dedicated to keep going, and have faith.

Oh, and by the way, you have to be humble and willing to learn.

OPENNESS TO NEW IDEAS AND EXPERIENCES

New ideas are scary. So are new experiences. We usually don't have a program for dealing with either. But if we're going to learn, we have to be open to both. It's a lot easier to cling to preconceptions. New ideas and experiences tend to shake us up. But unless you are already selling your copy, *being shaken up may be exactly what you need if you are to learn.*

It doesn't matter where you got your present preconceptions about what makes a "story," how you should write, what's "good" or "bad," or anything else. To be a professional and capable of growth, you have to junk your biases about what's good and bad in the craft. Even more important, you have to be willing to admit there are things you have yet to learn. You don't know everything—and you aren't as smart as you think—or you wouldn't be reading this book.

In teaching seminars on writing, I have often had the experience of going over some basic technique in agonizing detail and seeing a few people in the room yawning and looking impatient, as if (1) saying they already know this, or (2) thinking the point is irrelevant to them. Invariably these are the very people who prove on their next assignment that they didn't at all understand what was being said—and weren't smart enough to know they *needed* to know.

I once substitute-taught an ethics class to some very young children. I carefully went through several very basic ideas, outlining them on the blackboard. One little boy in the front row was staring into space, clearly bored and thinking about something else.

Finally I asked, "Are there any questions?" and to my great surprise this little boy's hand shot up.

"Yes, Joey?" I said expectantly.

Joey said, "We got a new puppy at my house."

Don't be a Joey. You might miss something.

The same open and receptive attitude must be maintained toward possible new experiences that can provide personal growth.

I have a good friend who was once a very successful writer. She decided she knew it all, and went into her Emily Dickinson configuration, holing up in the country, seeing few people, reading no new fiction, writing the same stuff.

Times changed.

Today, that immensely talented writer is unable to sell her copy. She writes like it's 1970 and she thinks like it's 1970 and she acts like it's 1970.

Do you think she would read current best-sellers to see what's going on? No. She doesn't like new novels, she says. Has she read any? No, she just knows she doesn't like them.

Do you think she would go to a popular dance club or attend a religious revival or date a new man or listen to a currently popular song or consider the viewpoint of an up-and-coming politician? No. None of that is any good, she says.

She is spending all her psychic energy fighting a futile back-door action against the only thing in the world that's certain: change. She has been left behind. She no longer knows the world, herself or the trade.

Creatively, she is dead. She can't sell her work today.

It takes honesty with yourself to see if you're like my friend. Think about it.

REJECTION OF VANITY AND PRETENSE

Snobbery and phony intellectualism have no place in a professional's attitude. Oh, it's comforting, I suppose, to posture, boast and deceive yourself about your own attainments and the supposed inferiority of others, but it's self-defeating.

I've met some so-called writers who strutted about, murmuring about the symbolic representation of unconscious paradigms, or some such. But they're never on the best-seller list. I've met others who figured they were really too smart and sophisticated to study technique. But they're never in a publisher's catalog.

Professional writers are people who work hard and study technique and get on with it. They don't bother themselves with trying to impress phonies.

WILLINGNESS TO WORK

Unfortunately, writing professionally is *hard work*. It's physically hard, sitting at that damned machine hour after hour. It involves long hours and a lot of drudgery. Sometimes you have to make the same mistake a hundred times before you finally see what you're doing wrong. Often, you have to stay on the job while everybody else is at play.

And as you were already warned, you have to give priority to this work. You have to make the effort when you feel well and when you're sick, when you're happy and when you're sad, when you're encouraged and when you're in the pits.

And when you're not writing, you often have to do research.

Research is sometimes fun, but seldom easy. It might involve countless hours in a library, searching for something you never do quite find. It might involve a trip through a muddy field in Missouri or a freezing night on the side of a mountain in Montana or a ghastly weekend with a couple of insufferable morons in an office in New York. It takes a physical toll on you. It is *not* play. But the professional pays the price.

COMMITMENT TO LONG-SUSTAINED EFFORT

A professional does not discourage easily.

For most writers, years of effort are required before anything gets published. Then, often more years have to pass before the product improves and better markets are within reach.

Also, a good novel may take two years to write, but only four hours to read. Most novels take more effort than nonwriters ever realize.

No professional will ever turn back from the long haul of his present project or the even more discouraging years that may lie ahead. If you're serious, you're in this for the duration.

And the duration is the rest of your life.

TRUST IN PROCESS

How can a writer face the long haul? By trusting in the process.

Sometimes when I face a writing class or seminar I feel a sense of uncertainty. Where does one start in trying to outline basic writing technique? One could start anywhere, for every technique relates to every other, and starting a seminar means pulling out one thread of this rich fabric, and then another . . .

and another . . . and hoping that somehow the description of each thread will lead the student finally to make a leap of intuition about the nature of the whole.

In *Zen in the Art of Archery*, by Eugen Herrigel, the student archer at first is allowed only to place the arrow on the bow preparatory to drawing the string. *And this minute bit of preparation is repeated for months*, no other step being taken. It is years, in this book, before the archer actually gets to shoot an arrow—and then he is told by the Zen master that he *never* shoots the arrow, but the arrow shoots itself when it is ready.

Learning to write is like this. You simply can't assimilate everything at once. It may be a long, long time before you know enough basics to be able to experience a flash of insight and say, "But of course! I see what narrative writing is all about!"

But, like the archer, to get there you must trust the process. You must study each technique in isolation, trusting that one day, if you persist long and hard enough, it will all come together for you.

Professionals in any endeavor know this. They don't expect shortcuts and easy answers. They chip away at the truth, knowing hard work will one day be rewarded. And the day your own synthesis takes place, you'll look up and say, "Of course!"

And those who haven't yet paid the price will say, "Oh, for you it's so easy!"

RESPECT FOR POPULAR CULTURE

I hesitate to use the term "popular culture" because it has a snobbish ring to it and the odor of book mold. But if we can trash the pseudo-intellectual connotations, it's a good term to describe writing, music, dance, and other art forms that are popular with the masses *today*.

You and I may be dismayed when we see a rock star wreck a guitar onstage or make unmusical noises and call it singing, or an athlete earn millions a year for shoving a ball through a hoop. We may see all kinds of things wrong and out of whack in our culture, which often rewards the bizarre and tasteless.

When we sit down to be professional writers, however, we have to fight the inclination to start making excuses for ourselves in the guise of "intelligent criticism" of popular culture. To sit around and bemoan the vulgarity of American society is a sure recipe for failure.

We live today. We have to sell our copy today. So we have to entertain today.

It may be comforting to sit around and tell ourselves—and others—that popular culture today is just too low-class for our own wonderfully intelligent and tasteful talent to blossom. But it's a chill comfort, and it won't keep your checkbook warm at night.

And it may not be true anyway. It's only in this century that the artificial distinction between "what's good" and "what's popular" began to be drawn by academics and their hoity-toity followers. From Chaucer to Shakespeare to Dickens, tale-tellers have worked in the frame of reference of common people, and have been popular with the person on the street. *There is nothing wrong with being popular and widely read. There is nothing wrong with wanting to reach a mass audience and make a buck while doing it.* Which would you prefer? To write something that you and five other esthetes think is wonderful—or to write something read and loved by millions? If you opted for the other five guys, you're reading the wrong book!

Does this mean you should sell out morally and intellectually, and write what you consider filth or trash? Of course not. Each of us has to make his own decision as to what he will write, how he will write it, and how far he will or won't go to try to draw an audience. I hope you have an artistic, creative conscience, and can draw your own line somewhere where it has meaning for you in terms of personal integrity.

But please don't fall into the trap of saying all popular fiction is junk, and that you are "above it." If you think that way, then your tastes and attitude need re-education—adjustment to reality.

Deal with the popular taste that exists. Where can your work fit? Don't—please!—sneer at everything on the new lists, everything on the best-seller racks, as trash.

For that way lies perdition.

COURAGE TO FACE OBSTACLES AND SETBACKS

A professional knows she will function day after day, month after month, up to her own average standard of performance.

But she also knows that everyone's work is uneven to some degree, that markets will change, that luck will change and that there will be wonderful ups and ghastly downs.

You have to persuade yourself that you'll cope over the long haul.

Writers begin with rejections, they live with rejections, and they die with rejections. Nobody sells everything.

It's hard to work when discouraged: hard to finish a book; hard to find an agent; hard to sell the manuscript; hard to accept the small advance and likely "publication in secret," with a sale so small you want to scream; hard to criticize your own work so you can grow; and hard to start the next project.

But you have to. If you're a pro, you simply accept these things and press on. Discouragement is a luxury you can't afford.

ENDURANCE (PHYSICAL AND SPIRITUAL)

The professional is tough and develops strength. Writing long hours is backbreaking physical work. You may have to hold multiple jobs, and find the strength to do your real work— your writing—late at night, when you're tired, when you feel half sick or discouraged. But that's part of the professional attitude. You'll do it.

You may even find that you have to force yourself to develop some "nonwriting" activities that nevertheless benefit your writing in indirect ways. One writer-friend of mine goes to a health club and works out three days a week to keep the body strong and to blow off the emotional steam that can build up from frustration at the word processor. Another friend has a canoe that gets frequent workouts. Another does woodworking. It's paradoxical, but sometimes to maintain the physical side of your endurance, you have to make your *nonwriting* schedule busier, too.

HOPE

Very often hope is all someone has to go on. But a professional never loses it.

AMBITION

I remember once in the early 1970s, after I had spent several years stuck on a plateau in my writing career, my editor at

Doubleday, Harold Kuebler, came to the University of Oklahoma for our annual writers' conference in June. The first evening, I drove him back to his motel and we talked for hours. Harold did most of the talking. He encouraged me, challenged me, goaded me, praised me—so excited me with renewed ambition that I didn't sleep the rest of the night. The result soon after was my embarking on the most ambitious book I had ever tried—a real breakthrough in my career.

The experience taught me something more about professionalism. You can never allow your ambition to gutter low. You have to cling to your original dream. And you must always have the fire in your belly, driving you to work harder and reach higher.

PATIENCE

This is still another attribute you have to have, to curb the pain of your ambition. It may take years to learn enough to start working like a professional. Years more to develop a career and a unique "voice." A single book may take a year or two out of your life and return little in the way of reward. Writing is a slow process. Revising is a slow process. Editorial decision-making is a slow process. *Then* you wait a year or more for the book to be published!

Slow down, be patient, take your time, check that research fact again, go on to the next project and stop stewing. Voices like these in your head are good voices, even if you hate them sometimes.

They're part of the professional approach, too.

HONESTY WITH ONESELF

Every writer has strengths and weaknesses. The pro has learned to locate her own weaknesses and work to strengthen them. She has also learned to recognize her strengths and capitalize on them.

Suppose you realize one day that your story dialogue is weak. You *don't* start saying, "Oh, woe is me, I'm no good!" And you certainly don't say, "All right, I'll just decide that the trend toward a lot of dialogue in books today is a bad thing, and I'll write without any dialogue in spite of the trend." What you *do* is find models, study them, practice, keep on criticizing yourself, and make yourself improve in the area of weakness you have discovered in yourself.

And if you also one day realize that you're great when dealing with character feelings, then don't just pat yourself on the back. Rather, look for stories and patterns that will let you get the maximum mileage out of your gift by writing stories where character feelings are dealt with in depth.

There is, however, another aspect of honesty. And that's learning to listen to your own inner voices—not kidding yourself about the kind of book you really enjoy reading, the kinds of feelings you really experience in your heart of hearts, the way you really *are* when all the defenses and pretenses you put up for the world every day have been taken down in the dark of night.

"Know thyself," the Greeks said, and there is no harder precept. But in your lifelong quest for professionalism, never lay down this part of your personal quest. The more you get in touch with your feelings and are honest with yourself about them, the better writer you can become.

COMPASSION

For a professional writer, compassion is a high-priority attribute. Luckily, it's also near the top of the "required list" for being a successful human being.

As a writer of fiction, you'll learn to observe people around you with greater interest and intensity than ever before. After all, those people are your grist. But you should never slip into cold, laboratory observation or analysis. These are *people* you're dealing with! Care about them. Feel with them. Get off your high horse and stop judging them all the time.

Have your own values, and never compromise them. But stop wasting your energy negatively judging and condemning others. Creative professionals have strong feelings, but don't put people in pigeonholes or issue sweeping indictments.

Put yourself in others' places. Imagine their plight. Fight to feel as they do, for a change. *Really listen* to them.

On this point, it's a proven fact that most of us don't really listen. During most conversations we're either off somewhere else, mentally, or we're already shutting the other person off after a few words because we're busy starting to formulate our response.

Psychologists often encourage troubled couples to practice really listening. They have the man, say, talk first. When he is finished, the woman is told to feed back to the man exactly what he just said. Amazingly, most people fail this test miserably. What was sent is usually *not* what was heard. (And when the woman talks first, it's invariably just as bad.)

Luckily, it doesn't take a lot of practice to become a better listener-observer. All you have to do is feed back to the speaker what has just been said to you. You say, "If I understand you, you're saying. . . ." (paraphrasing the factual content).

Once you get the hang of it, you'll be a better partner in any situation. You'll also have started to trash some of those preconceptions and conversational gambits that may have stopped you, all your life, from really observing people around you.

HARD-HEADED PRACTICALITY

Despite the dreams of winning every tournament, taking every prize, becoming wealthy and famous and making history, the professional attitude is always tempered by practicality.

At whatever stage you may be in your career, you must guard against allowing the dream to drive you to overreach yourself. The professional always fights to improve, but he compromises to the extent of seeing realistically what is possible *now*. One accepts one's limitations and works within them at the same time one studies and practices to improve.

You need to deal with the realities of publishing, too. I've had students who almost had a nervous breakdown because an editor kept a manuscript two months before rendering a verdict. Long delays are normal—three months' waiting time isn't even a long delay. And if you catch yourself saying things like, "I wouldn't accept an offer from a mere paperback publisher," or "If they offer only $10,000, I would rather just keep the manuscript in my attic," you're living in never-never land, not the real world of publishing.

ATTENTION TO CURRENT MODELS

One of the main things wrong with many college writing programs today is that all the attention is paid to classical models—Tolstoy, Conrad, Dickens, and the great Americans from the early part of the twentieth century. Of course you can learn tremendously from studying such writers, but it's axiomatic that many of the past greats might not even get their books sold today. The market, and reader tastes, have changed that much.

Given such a reality, the professional writer studies *current* successes. He asks himself why such-and-such a novel was a success, and he never allows subjective judgment or jealousy to enter into his evaluation. *It doesn't really matter whether you happen to like the best-seller at hand or not.* The point is that it *is* a best-seller. And you don't really want to write failures that end up in the bottom desk drawer, do you?

In paying attention to current models, the professional analyzes for every conceivable technique and angle. This time it may be to analyze dialogue, next time it might be to see all the different ways characters are introduced, and the next time something else.

Whether you personally happen to like the writer's approach may be quite irrelevant. If a lot of people out there did like it, what can you learn from it that you might apply to your own work?

Many times in the pages that follow, I'll suggest that you analyze copy to see the technique under discussion in action. It's easy to read right past such suggestions. That's what an *amateur*—doomed to remain one—will do.

If you study current models and force yourself to be really alert for technique, you may be surprised sometimes to notice new things about writing fiction that you never suspected before. All any book or course can give you is a learner's permit. Writers really are made by studying about techniques and attitudes, then writing (and often failing), then studying and analyzing—tearing apart, diagramming, coding and marking up—published contemporary copy, and then trying again.

Attention to current models and analysis thereof should be a lifelong pursuit for you.

ACCEPTANCE OF CHANGE

What worked yesterday may not work today. Audiences are changing. Markets change, too. So do values and public perceptions and writing styles. Don't fight it. Be aware of what's going on *today* and tailor your copy accordingly.

DETERMINATION TO GROW

Every professional wants to get better, no matter how good he may be at present. Even when you're working on a project that seems within your present capabilities—even while you're being realistic *and* patient—you may also find yourself writing other private projects designed to test new techniques and stretch you as an artist. Good.

Don't forget those new experiences you need to be open to. They'll stretch you, too. Travel seldom fails to fire up a writer.

WILLINGNESS TO RISK

There are two kinds of risk for a writer: trying new techniques and fields of writing, and revealing oneself.

The first has been covered. The second may be harder.

Whatever you write is, in some small way, going to reveal the kind of person you are, the state of your feelings, what you believe, etc. That's inevitable. So self-revelation should not frighten you, and it doesn't scare the professional; she accepts it, and dares to walk close to the abyss of sentimentality or other emotional excess. Feelings are the nucleus of good fiction. You must deal with them—in yourself and in your copy.

That's one of the reasons writing fiction is so tiring, and it's something nonwriters never quite understand. Writing a strong, emotional scene is a harrowing, exhausting experience. But it's something you can't dodge if you want to excel.

REFUSAL TO MAKE EXCUSES

A long time ago, on one of the first plays in a National Football League title game, Sammy Baugh, the great passer for the Washington Redskins, threw a long bomb intended for a wide receiver—who dropped the ball in the open. The other team went on to destroy the Redskins by a score of something like 73-0.

After the game, a reporter asked Baugh if the outcome might have been different if that first pass had been caught.

Slingin' Sammy responded, "Yes. It would have been 73-7."

That's the professional attitude. No excuses, no blaming of luck or trends or somebody else's stupidity. No pretending that the game was below his talents or that he didn't really want it anyway.

Real pros don't waste energy—or short-circuit their own efforts—by complaining, making excuses, or otherwise avoiding reality.

The reality is that you'll sell if you're good enough. Pretending otherwise is baloney.

VERBAL EXCELLENCE

Do you find it strange that we would list verbal writing skills so far down in a list of what makes a professional writer? You shouldn't. I simply assume that you can already write good, clean, grammatical copy. Verbal felicity is basic in the writer's toolbox. It's a given. If you have trouble with faulty parallelisms, dangling participles, comma splices or anything else of that nature—or if you don't know what such things are—you are probably wasting your time trying to be a professional writer. That kind of ability is where you start.

Your style should be clean, transparent, invisible—a pane through which the reader experiences the story.

UNQUENCHABLE PERFECTIONISM

Don't ever tell yourself that your copy, your story or (above all) your effort are "good enough." For that way lies compromise with the best that you can be, and as a professional you can never be satisfied with less than total effort, preoccupation, persistence and performance.

Even in the matter of the appearance of your submitted copy you must be a perfectionist. If you don't already know about professional manuscript requirements, there are any number of publications that can tell you everything you need to know on the subject.

♦♦♦

Discouraged? I hope not. The professional attitudes listed are common to all successful novelists. And those people are your competition. If you think and work like a professional too, you can compete with them on a level playing field.

It's unlikely you'll ever stumble upon a novice contest in commercial publishing. You may be able to win a writers' club competition despite amateurish mistakes, but you aren't likely to go much further.

So let me suggest that you take a short break from reading now and make notes in your journal about what being a professional means to you. What in your lifestyle, attitudes or work habits has not been professional? What do you plan to do about it? What? You don't have a work journal? Start one! Force yourself to do this. It's the professional thing to do. Make notes, analyze yourself, come up with work and study plans, and get it all written down in the journal. Start *doing* things the right, disciplined way, rather than daydreaming about it.

Once you're caught up with that assignment, come back here. In the next chapter we'll start building on that new attitude of yours.

Chapter Two

Work Habits
and the Imagination

Occasionally someone asks if writing freelance articles or working full time for a newspaper or advertising agency is inimical to writing fiction. The answer is that no such other activity will hurt you if you have enough determination and stamina to do your real work regularly. Further, the work discipline learned in a profession such as journalism may even help.

The reason newspaper work, for example, may help is that journalists learn (1) to create on the typewriter or word processor; (2) to write on a moment's notice, not waiting for "inspiration," and (3) to work almost anywhere.

They're all important things to learn.

Everyone is different. If you find that you have to write things out longhand before revising on a keyboard, there's nothing wrong with that. But chances are good that you may be tricking yourself into taking an extra step in the process of getting final copy ready to show an editor, in effect "warming up your motor" with the longhand version and being too easy on yourself until later.

Most professionals teach themselves to compose on the keyboard. With the advent of computers, later revision then means having copy that you can fix already on the disk, rather than having to key it in all over again—a valuable time-saver. It also means that the imagination *knows* somehow from the first keystroke that this is serious business. So it's good to teach yourself to compose at the keyboard. To learn to do that, you start doing it. The more you do it, the easier it gets.

WRITING TO A REGULAR QUOTA–NOW

The professional writer can almost always "turn it on" on demand, on a moment's notice. He has to be able to do this if he is to maintain production over time.

There's no reason why anyone should sit around, worry, agonize and manage to write only a page or two of copy per day. I've never known a writer with such a low production level who didn't spend most of his time staring into space when he was supposed to be putting words on paper. Journalistic work, with pressing deadlines, forces you to write now, not later. But if you don't have a newsroom or agency to work in, you can force your own imagination to produce on demand simply by doing it.

Wherever you plan to write, and whenever, the important thing is to make sure you have a quota of words or pages that you *will* produce at each sitting before you allow yourself to get up and do something else. As I said in chapter one, if you sit down at your machine with the idea of spending two hours, that's just what you'll do—spend two hours. And since the imagination is a lazy muscle, most of the two hours will be spent staring, worrying, thinking about other things and being frightened and frustrated.

If you sit down knowing you are going to stay right there until you've produced, say, five pages, then you'll quickly begin to learn to produce pages on demand, without a lot of waiting for inspiration and wasteful daydreaming.

It helps a lot of writers, they say, to have a regular, sacrosanct place for the task. If you can have a dedicated workplace, great, but having a production quota is more important.

The first job of any writer, especially the novelist, is the production of pages. Any pages are better than no pages. Once you have some copy in the box, you can fix it later. If you're sitting around waiting for inspiration to strike, you're not producing anything but frustration for yourself.

The more you get into the groove of regular production, three or five or ten pages a day, at least five days a week, the easier you'll find it is to produce. That's not only because you'll be developing the habit of writing, it's also because nothing feeds work like previous work.

WORK MAKES EVERYTHING RELEVANT

Another facet, however, that may be more important is the fact that even when you're unaware of it, the imagination and the unconscious mind will concentrate on an ongoing creative project, once that project is rolling. Simply being at work facilitates the work.

A friend once told this story: "I was halfway through a long novel project," he said, "and was having trouble with one of the major characters. I simply could not figure out what kind of person he was. Then, by necessity, I had to take a short business trip.

"On the airplane, I met a man who seemed jovial, easygoing, and a lot of fun to be with. He even helped the cabin attendants serve drinks, and he had everyone in my section of the plane laughing.

"As he handed me my drink, however, our eyes happened to meet for a moment. His eyes were like steel bearings.

"That instant of eye contact gave me a jolt. It dawned on me that here was a man whose jovial exterior was an act, part of a carefully crafted professional facade designed to put people off guard, possibly so he could take advantage of them.

"And in the same instant I knew he had given me the key to my character in the novel. I went home after the trip and made the 'problem character' one of the best I've ever created."

What does the story prove? Simply this: Because the writer was preoccupied at some level with the character in his book, the interesting man on the airplane immediately became relevant to the writer's creative problem. And so, without having to think about it, the writer was receptive to stimuli that would help him with his solution. Once he had a novel under way, everything became relevant to that project. He didn't have to hunt consciously. He had put himself in a frame of mind where the solutions would come. If the writer had not been working on the book when he took his trip, that moment's eye contact with the other traveler would have slipped away, never to be used.

That's the way it works, once you have a book under way. Everything is relevant. Everything is grist. Ideas come. Connections become apparent. And all because of the preoccupation that comes from steady, disciplined involvement with the project.

ONCE WRITTEN, IT CAN BE FIXED

There are other reasons why it's so vital to have a project under way, and to be working on it with great regularity and production-quota discipline.

One of them is that good novels aren't written—they're rewritten. Few writers can predict what sort of changes may be necessary in a given segment after other parts of the story have been written. Characters may change. Plants may be required. Plot assumptions may go out the window. Timing may be altered.

So why should you agonize over every word of a first draft, or stare out the window awaiting inspiration? It all may change later anyway. Remember that your everyday production will make the imagination function better as you go along. It's almost inevitable that you'll be producing so much better a few weeks from now—and imagining so much more vividly—that you'll want to go back to revise earlier work anyway.

Produce pages today! Everything else will follow.

OTHER AIDS TO THE IMAGINATION

There are two more ways to stimulate the imagination that might be worth mentioning: list-making and meditation. Neither is a substitute for regular, quota-oriented, backbreaking labor. But they may help.

The human brain, as you probably know, is divided into two hemispheres, left and right. The left hemisphere deals with logic, language processing and mathematics. The right hemisphere is the seat of feelings, imagination, creativity and intuition. The two hemispheres communicate with each other, but imperfectly.

Thus, writing a novel is an uneasy alliance. The right hemisphere provides the inspiration, the pictures in your mind, the dialogue flow and the all-important feelings. The left hemisphere provides the story logic, the planning, the analysis and the words.

All well and good—but what happens when the left hemisphere's logical patterns interfere with what the wonderful right hemisphere is trying to do? What can you do when the left hemisphere starts sternly censoring ideas from the right—when that too-logical little voice in your head says, "That's corny," or "That's so dumb"?

One way to get more ideas—from plot topics to character decisions to developmental twists—is to work the right hemisphere, the imagination, so fast that it doesn't have time to listen to the nagging criticisms of the left. You do this by making lists. Speedy lists.

Suppose in your story that Joe just got Mary to accept his proposal of marriage. Now you want Joe to have an unpredictable and interesting reaction to her acceptance. You have thought—carefully and logically—of several possibilities, but none of them really turns you on, and several times your left hemisphere critic has kept you from writing down an idea by saying, even as the idea surfaced, "That's dumb!"

So the left critic is fighting the right creator, and you're stuck.

What to do? Make a list. *Just as swiftly as you can,* and with absolutely no thought as to rationality or corniness or any of that other bad left-hemisphere stuff, write down twenty reactions Joe might have. Fast!

If you are willing to go along with me and try it, make your list before you proceed here. If you'll take the time to do this—and make your list very swiftly, refusing to censor yourself and putting down *whatever* crazy idea pops up next—I guarantee you'll come up with some interesting results.

What happens in such cases is that the imagination first sends up routine, easy ideas. Then, forced to send up more—something—*anything*—it freewheels and the results get wild and wonderful. So the faster you list and the more steadfastly you refuse to hang up and "stop to think"—all of which is limiting left-hemisphere activity—the better your list will become.

In creativity workshops, I often demonstrate this by holding up a chalkboard eraser and asking the participants to list ten ways in which the object could be used as a murder weapon. This exercise sounds absurd enough (a ploy on my part to start defusing the left-hemisphere censor), and it gets more interesting when I tell the participants they have ninety seconds to write down their list of ten methods.

Some people write two or three ideas and frown, staring into space. They just lost. Some pause between each item and scratch out and revise. They lost, too. A few write furiously for five or six easy items, then go blank. They also failed. A few others dig in and just scribble down any kind of *junk* that pops into their mind. Of this small number, almost always there is someone who looks up suddenly with this incredible pained and almost embarrassed expression, then writes furiously, perhaps with a grimace.

I call on the "losers" first, asking for best solutions. The results are always predictable—make the eraser a projectile, somehow, or hit someone on the head with it, or push it down the victim's throat, or put it at the top of the stairs and make the victim fall over it.

Those who pushed themselves harder often come up with stuff that's more creative, such as grinding the thing up and poisoning soup with it somehow, or using it to plug a filter in the victim's vital life-support system (which shows how the unbridled inagination can instantly invent all kinds of ancillary story ideas). But it's the ones in the group who feverishly completed a list of *all ten* ideas who come up with the best things. And of these, I save that person who looked up with an incredulous expression until the very last.

One of the most interesting ideas I ever got from this last group was from a man who looked embarrassed when he said, "You use the eraser to *rub the victim out.*"

People groaned. I was stunned, then delighted. The imagination had leaped to an entirely different level of thinking, a thoroughly abstract, symbolic level. *Forced* to keep freewheeling without time for the left hemisphere to interfere, it had done something wondrously creative.

So try list-making! At worst you'll come up with something on paper that you can ponder, instead of a blank page and a blank mind with the left hemisphere critic cackling in the background. At best you'll amaze yourself.

MEDITATION

Another method of increasing your imaginative power lies in meditative technique. You don't need to make a big issue of this. All you need is a few minutes' quiet time and a comfortable place to sit.

Relax and close your eyes. Imagine a pleasant place . . . a lakeside or a mountain glen. Imagine the feel of the wind, the look of the white clouds against the vivid blue of the sky, the scent of water and grass, the sigh of the wind in nearby trees, the feel of your body relaxing and letting go. If some more "logical" thought comes along from your left hemisphere, just watch it drift across your mind and go out again.

Relax . . . enjoy . . . see, taste, feel, hear, smell things in your quiet place of escape . . . and drift. After a little while, when you're ready, slowly open your eyes. When you feel like doing so, stretch and yawn. Come back slowly.

If you do this as little as ten minutes in the evening, you will find that creative energy is increased. You may see colors more vividly the next day, or notice an enhanced sharpness and vibrancy in music, or make a new mental connection of some kind. You may sleep better and awaken more refreshed, or uncover new sources of energy. You definitely will notice some signs that this simple exercise has rejuvenated your imagination and made it freer and more ready to work for you.

Notice your favorite color in your favorite fantasy. What is it? Stop and write it down, now.

A SUMMARY REVIEW

So let's recap ideas to enhance your creativity.

Have a regular place and time to work if you can.
Work at least five days a week.
Have a production quota.
Make lists.
Meditate.

As we move along, other ideas for aiding your imagination will be suggested in connection with various techniques. But these are the basics—and there is no basic more fundamental than hard, ongoing work.

GIVING NEW IDEAS "SOAK TIME"

One more idea should be mentioned. It's simply this: Sometimes when learning new things, you need to give your mind enough time to ponder what has just been presented. It's almost as if your brain is a sponge, and it requires a bit of time to let the new stuff soak in.

My writing lectures are designed, for example, to have the students do exercises to anchor every technique that has been taught. But just as important is the "soak time" that will allow the new learning to percolate from the left hemisphere, where it's artificial and logical and therefore not very helpful, into the right hemisphere, where it does wonderful things.

I can't build in soak time for you. But I can suggest that you pause and think about your own work habits and imagination; if you can, come up with some ideas on how to improve your productivity. Make a list and add it to your journal.

Then relax a while, close your eyes and think about that favorite color you just noted a few minutes ago. Don't charge into the next chapter until you've given your noggin time to absorb and synthesize a little. Wait till tomorrow, or the day after that.

But in the meantime, it's OK to produce some pages.

Chapter Three

The Nature of Story

Years ago, a popular novelist was asked what kind of a writer he considered himself to be. He said, "I practice the discipline of the narrative."

The interviewer didn't seem to get it. But every writer of stories—every tale-teller—in the history of the world would have understood the answer at once.

There was a time when most people would have understood the assumptions implied in the novelist's reply. But lately, thanks to the artificial distinction made in this century between popular fiction and fiction considered "good" by academicians, confusion is everywhere. It's made worse by the increasingly frantic scurrying after the bizarre and incredible by some fiction editors who seemingly will fall for anything that seems "different" enough. Some readers, numbed by the sensationalism of crashing airplanes and flying bullets on TV, applaud and compound the chaos.

But dedication to chaos and weirdness doesn't help you much when you're trying to write a narrative likely to sell.

Luckily, professional writers still know what the discipline of the narrative is, and if you're interested in making money as a novelist, you can learn it too.

My former teacher Dwight V. Swain used to say that a story could be defined as "the formed record of a character-testing conflict told from a viewpoint." That sounds simple enough. I offer it to you as a shorthand overview of the storytelling process.

But be warned: Every word in Swain's definition is loaded and used in a specialized way.

STORY AS FORMED RECORD

The first key word in Swain's definition is "formed." It implies author control of his material, a formal pattern, consciousness by the author of narrative principles, and adherence to classical dramatic structure.

Good stories do not just happen. There is a very logical progression in the formation of any story. A good story:

- begins with the establishment of someone confronted by a change that is threatening to that person's self-concept;
- proceeds to the formation of a goal essential to that person's happiness in response to the threatening change;
- provides dramatic events played onstage in the story "now" in a logical but unanticipated sequence founded in reversal of expectation;
- builds to a climax involving moral dilemma;
- finds resolution in sacrifice;
- provides demonstration of theme in an ultimate outcome not easily predicted by the reader, but deeply satisfying in the "but, of course" irony of the ending.

Some of that seems awfully hard to digest, but it's important. It represents a capsule version of almost every chapter in the remainder of this book. Keep it in the back of your mind, and by the end of this book you'll see how much storytelling logic lies behind every phrase.

OTHER VIEWS ... BUT NO ACCIDENTS

Others have begun their definition of "story" with different assumptions. In his book, *The Basic Formulas of Fiction*, William Foster-Harris, one of my predecessors at the University of Oklahoma, said a story could always be defined by way of an equation identifying the abstract principles at war in the story. Foster-Harris, in other words, would have "defined" a story of a priest in love with a woman as an equation:

religious devotion + sexual love = ?

I prefer to think of story more in terms of the dramatic working out of an external conflict in the plot action which shows and worsens the conflict inside the character. And others have stated it other ways.

The point, however, is that no serious fiction theoretician suggests that a story is an accident. This is why our definition begins with the demand that the story must be formed by the author, not by chance. Several of the chapters that follow will relate to formation and control of "story," as opposed to the idea that a story sometimes happens by some process of alchemy.

CHARACTER-TESTING CONFLICT

When Swain speaks of a "character-testing conflict," every word is loaded. For example, when a professional writer speaks of "character," that single word includes so many assumptions that the mind boggles. A "character" in fiction is many things.

In the first place, a character is *not* a real person. Real people, when rendered with total fidelity on paper, are dull, unconvincing and vague. A fiction character must, first of all, be a host of exaggerations.

Why? Because one of the hardest things we ask readers to do is to take some symbols on a piece of paper, translate these symbols into words, process the words into meanings, sort out and react to both the denotation and connotation of those words (not to mention deep processing of secondary associations!), then take all this and imagine a human being, then believe the human being actually exists—but in a make-believe world—identify with the person, care about the person, worry about the person and invest time in finding out what happens to that person—who doesn't really exist anywhere except in the imagination!

Readers understandably aren't very good at this.

It's as if I were to introduce you to someone in real life, but the two of you were separated by a very large pane of smoked glass. I might stand a real individual, in her normal clothing and makeup, on my side of the smoke-darkened panel. She would be *real* in every detail. You, however, trying to see her through the panel, would get only the vaguest, most shadowy and unconvincing perception. You wouldn't see her at all clearly.

What to do?

In order to make you believe you were seeing a real person, I would have to exaggerate her greatly: a bright orange dress and fluorescent red shoes; chalk on her skin; bright crimson lipstick around her mouth; inky covering of her eyebrows and around her nose. And if she were to talk (since it would be hard for you to hear, too), she would have to shout.

Your impression, seeing through the glass, darkly, now would be to perceive what looked like a normal, credible person. You would say, "Great! What a real person this is!"

When we use the word "character" in defining a story, we have this kind of exaggeration in mind to make the struggling reader believe in the character at all. In addition to exaggeration, we use other devices in order to be convincing. (Many of these other devices will be examined in chapters five, twelve and thirteen.)

For now, the important thing to remember is that a story character is anything but a real person and must be based on exaggeration, which only begins with accurate observation of real-life people.

THE NATURE OF A "TEST"

Even the word "testing" in our working definition of story is a loaded concept. Consider what a "test" is all about. It's a confrontation, a crisis, a genuine trying-out, and not just an idle stroll through an accidental afternoon. Tests are active, with give-and-take, and they have serious implications and detectable results, good or bad.

And what about the word "conflict"? Many people have trouble with conflict. They spend their lives trying to avoid it. Conflict, for many, is always unpleasant and stressful. "Better to give up or avoid it," you might say. Not in fiction!

Conflict—the struggle between story characters over clear, stated goals—is the engine force of fiction. It's what makes most stories work. It's possible to write stories of discovery or decision in which the conflict is internal, inside the character's head, but most successful stories put the conflict outside, between story people, fighting onstage in the story "now."

CONFLICT MUST BE FACED

Don't, please, succumb to the temptation of being "subtle" and having all the conflict only inside your character if you can possibly avoid it. It is enormously more difficult to interest your reader that way.

Imagine: How dramatic will it be if you put your conflict all inside the character and sit her onstage? There she is, your heroine, poor Matilda, sitting on the bench in the spotlight, stage center. The audience of thousands is hushed. You, the author, know Matilda is experiencing inner conflict.

What does the audience get? Nothing. Matilda just sits there, possibly occasionally twitching or shedding a tear. The theater audience goes home. "Crummy story," they all agree. "Wait a minute!" you scream at the empty seats. "There was a lot of neat conflict here! It was just all inside her!" A critic comes back for his forgotten hat. "Sorry," he tells you. "We couldn't see it."

Get the message? Conflict is a fight at some level, and it takes two onstage to have it. It doesn't matter how much you dearly love your long, interior monologues or masterfully disguised personal essays about the state of God and the Universe. Readers want conflict! You have to face that, and provide it.

Notice, too, that *conflict is not the same as adversity.*

Adversity is bad luck. It's fate. It's blind.

Joe leaves his apartment in the morning. He's late because his clock stopped. He trips going to his car and skins his knee. The battery in his car has died overnight and he has to take the bus. On the bus he gets mugged. He staggers into his office just as the building catches fire. Poor Joe.

But a reader needs to feel more than sympathy for a character. Adversity may build sympathy, but it will never build admiration or concern.

And adversity is blind. When Joe heads home tonight, a tree in the park is going to fall on him and break his back, and then by more bad luck his ambulance is going to ram into a bread truck.

Joe can't fight adversity. He has no chance. Adversity is blind, and will come or go by luck, no matter what Joe does or doesn't do. In a universe of adversity, nothing makes sense—nothing Joe does will make any difference.

It's very difficult to hold a reader with nothing but blind fate playing all the cards. The story may be exciting in places, but it tends to be meaningless.

On the other hand, if you give Joe a goal, and have someone else oppose him, the reader can take sides and care. So let's have Joe get to work, march into his boss's office and demand a raise, saying a raise is vital to his happiness. His boss argues. They struggle verbally.

Now we're getting somewhere! Whatever happens *will happen in part as a result of Joe's own actions.* The story world will begin to make more sense than life usually does—be better than life—because here, at least, people get what they get as a result of how they act.

This, in a nutshell, is why fiction is better than life. It makes more sense. It's also why we have fiction at all. If it was really as random as real life, we wouldn't like it—wouldn't have it. It's why conflict beats adversity, six ways from Sunday. And why you must recognize the difference—and use conflict.

THE USE OF VIEWPOINT

Every story is someone's story. Each one of us lives in his own unique universe.

Joe and Arnold and Sam may live what seem to be identical experiences. But the viewpoint of each—his world and how he experiences it—will be unique, totally different from any other.

This is one reason why fiction must proceed from a viewpoint. We make it possible for the reader to experience the story through the eyes and ears and heart and mind of a character who is *inside the action, participating in the story and vitally concerned with its outcome.*

There are a lot of other reasons why viewpoint is essential to fiction. The reader needs to identify with someone, "root for" someone, experience the story in the way she experiences her own real life, and believe in the make-believe.

We'll talk a lot more about this in chapter five. Right now, we're doing an overview. The primary point is—again—that viewpoint is part of a construct by the author. Again, not an accident.

STORY AS MOVEMENT

So we are almost ready to move from story definition to another aspect of storytelling. Before we do, however, there is one more aspect of story that must be mentioned to anyone thinking of writing a novel. And that is the matter of *movement*.

It's possible to write short fiction with very little movement. But in a novel, movement—development of events—is everything. In a novel, not only must there be many more events than you perhaps have dreamed of, but *events must have downstream effects*.

This is such a basic point that it can hardly be overstressed. Unfortunately, it also appears so simple—and is so close to the magical center of understanding narrative fiction—that you might work years before you fully appreciate its significance.

Novels may include many, many incidents—little happenings that come and go and are thought no more about. A shoeshine boy is seen at the curb; horns honk; a storm blows in. And perhaps none of these incidents has a downstream effect.

But if a reader is to be carried along through a long narrative, he must believe that (1) what you're presenting now has genuine significance in the final working-out of the novel (else why would he bother to read this page of your book?), and (2) this story world does make sense, and effects have causes—causes lead to effects.

So—again (and again)—a novel comes out better than life. Scene A is played, and somehow it results in Scene B (or Scene X!); Scene B, when it plays, is relevant, and also has downstream effects in the novel. The reader is rushed along, the narrative movement sustaining and heightening his interest, and the yarn gets played out with a grand intensity and an ironic logicality that puts real life in the shade.

Of course very short stories may not demonstrate this aspect of fiction. As a matter of fact, most of us tend to start out not writing stories at all, but vignettes.

You know what a vignette is: it's the English department's much-beloved "slice of life," a moment in time, strong on mood, probably striking, preciously written.

Here's one:

> Night. The waterfront. Out of the fog comes the sound of a lonely foghorn in the bay. There is a street, cobbles, with shabby buildings. The fog makes halos around the streetlamps. Puddles glisten blackly. There is an empty

bus bench facing across the dreary street to a little diner, where, behind the sweaty glass, are light and laughter.

Enter stage right a little old man in a long raincoat. He shuffles to the window of the cafe, looks in, appears sad. He sighs. Exits stage left. The foghorn sounds.

Wonderful.

But nothing has happened. No character, no viewpoint, no conflict, no downstream effects—nothing. If you want to make it in this business, and if you've been writing stuff like the above, quit! And *don't*, please, imagine that you can fix this kind of faulty fictional approach with a couple of tricks. For example, by rewriting the above something like the following:

> Night. The waterfront. Out of the fog comes the sound of a lonely foghorn in the bay. There is a street, cobbles, with shabby buildings. The fog makes halos around the streetlamps. Puddles glisten blackly. There is an empty bus bench facing across the dreary street to a little diner, where, behind the sweaty glass, are light and laughter.
>
> Julie walked to the bench and sat down, tired and lonely. *(This is great! Now I have a viewpoint character!)*
>
> Enter stage right a little old man in a long raincoat. He shuffles to the window of the cafe, looks in, appears sad. He sighs. Julie thinks, "I'll go over there and offer that little old man a cup of coffee and make him happier." *(Wonderful! A goal!)* Julie crosses the street, speaks to the old man. He opens his raincoat and exposes himself to her, and exits stage left. The foghorn sounds.
>
> *(Uh-oh! Something went wrong here!)*

You see? Tricks won't replace movement. The vignette has remained dead-ended, even with the gimmick.

There will be more later about downstream effects, cause and effect, and movement, too. We look at various aspects of these essential elements in chapters six through nine and again in chapter sixteen. But for now, at least take an initial step. Make a note in your journal (and perhaps a note over your word processor): *Keep it moving.*

Which means, keep things happening. Invent more *events*— developments which cause other developments later downstream in your novel. Keep your characters active, not passive. Never let up. Maintain speedy development.

For in today's markets, more than ever before, swift movement is vital. The novelist who tries to survive on mood and tricks very likely will never get published. Indeed, there are days when I think movement is everything.

Again, you should stop to think a bit about all of this. Then make notes in your work journal summarizing the points given in this chapter. Reread some of your own recent fiction; are you following the precepts outlined here? If not, what can you do about it? Make your notes and plans a part of your journal too.

Chapter Four

Show Me First!

The last of the bedrock general principles we need to establish before moving into more specific techniques is one that goes to reader orientation. In its simplest terms, the underlying truth here is this: The reader of your novel has to be kept aware of *where* the action is taking place, *when* it's happening, *who* is involved and *what* is going on.

It's vital, too, for the reader to understand *why* something is happening.

Those of you with journalistic training will recognize the traditional "Five Ws" said to be essential in every complete news story. In journalism, the reporter is urged to remember these five Ws in order to produce a total rendition of the facts as known. In the novel, your job is to provide the same basics to keep the reader from being hopelessly confused about the events you're trying to portray.

It sounds simple. It can be. Often, however, it isn't.

Why? Because writers so very often fail to distinguish between what they're seeing in their imagination as they write, and what they are actually putting down on paper for the reader to see. (And, of course, when I use the word "see," I also mean "hear," "feel," "smell," etc.)

The result of such unintended negligence by the inexperienced novelist: Scenes that are confusing at best, disorienting or totally meaningless at worst.

A student of mine in an adult writing class provided a classic example of the problem we're addressing here. She was writing a historical romance set in Elizabethan England. Now, it's axiomatic that such a historical romance must be rich in period detail—costumes, houses, castles, ships, candelabras, carriages—all the stuff that can make such a book a wonderful transportation into another physical world full of exotic things and experiences.

My student, however, was confronted very early in the book with a sequence of events in which the heroine awoke in a castle where she was visiting, dressed, went downstairs to the courtyard where knights on horseback were waiting, got into a carriage, rode through a woods and a moor to the docks of London, and boarded a seafaring schooner.

Great! The trouble is, she wrote the entire sequence in not many more words than I used in condensing the action here. She gave me no description. She didn't even tell me it was morning when the scene started. She told me nothing at all about what the young woman viewpoint character was thinking or feeling.

The result was confusion on my part—and boredom.

After a couple of discussions about it, my student went off and revised the sequence of events several times. What finally came back to me, thank goodness, was marvelous. It was filled with dank castle walls at dawn; a thin sun trying to break through a chill fog; the heroine's fear and nervousness and uncertainty, and anxiety to reach the ship; a cold cobblestone courtyard filled with gaunt men in chain armor astride prancing horses with steam rising from their hot backs; the jostling of the carriage wheels on a rough rock road; a grim forest where the giant trees made the day seem like night; a foggy moor with ghostly stumps standing in black water; and finally a ride down a city street to the dock, with its smell of the sea, great sailing ships standing in the mist, the clamor of sailors' voices and creaking of winches loading cargo—and the rising tumult of fear as the gangplank was lowered and our heroine went on board.

I was, as a reader, transported back to that time, thrust into a strange and captivating world and tremendously entertained. I was ready to identify with the viewpoint character and believe whatever plot developments took place next.

The writer and I talked about it after she had done so well.

"I saw and felt that stuff the first time I wrote it," she told me apologetically. "I just forgot to put it in."

Exactly.

YOU CAN OVERDO IT

Does this example mean that you should shovel in mountains of adjectives and adverbs—steamy streams of words—at every opportunity? Of course not. You can overdo reader orientation of this kind. The result can be pages of lifeless "purple prose" guaranteed to revolt any sensitive reader while the story comes to a screeching halt. But for every student writer I encounter who badly overdoes it, I meet a dozen who forget, just as this student did.

So *don't* pour on the juicy, purple description. But remember that the reader has to be put into the scene. You must provide enough concise, evocative detail to let the reader imagine the rest for herself. Which means, probably, that you may first write in too much description and mention of character feelings, but then trim them back, honing every word, to provide just enough sharply suggestive detail.

Some aspects of this task can be daunting. As a matter of fact, I've written an entire book on the subject. (*Setting*, published by Writer's Digest Books.) In this chapter, however, we're talking general principles that should always be remembered. And the general principle might be restated this way: *Be sure to show the reader enough of what you're seeing in your imagination.*

Remember that for now, and make some notes about it in your journal. We'll come back to it in chapter ten for more detail.

SCENE OPENERS AND STAGE ACTION

The kind of reader orientation issue discussed above is only one aspect of the five Ws, however. After all, not everyone is writing a historical romance where rich evocation is mandatory. You may be the kind of writer who wants to produce a lean, spare story of crime and detection, where lush description is practically unheard of. In that case you may seldom have to go to great lengths to set a scene, although you will still have to provide enough detail to put the reader into the story world.

In your case, and perhaps in the cases of most new novelists, the problem of reader orientation takes a slightly different form. In any novel, almost every time a new scene opens after a time break or change in locale, the novelist *must* make sure to reorient the reader on all the five Ws. (The only exception would be the very occasional situation where you, the writer, *want* the reader to be confused.)

To clarify this, let's assume that in your imagination you see Brad, the hero, in his apartment at midnight. There is a knock on the door and Brad, sleepy and wearing pajamas, goes to the door, opens it, sees his fiancee Jill standing there upset and disheveled, invites her in, and, feeling great concern, hugs her and asks her to sit down on the couch and tell him what's wrong.

Good. Unfortunately, I have often seen such a simple sequence of events become impenetrable just because the writer left out too many small details that I, the reader, had to have.

For example, it might be (badly) written something like this.

> The doorbell rang. She looked terrible.
> "Come in. What's wrong?"
> "It's awful."
> "Tell me."

If you had read these four lines at the opening of a new chapter in a novel—without benefit of the description of writer assumptions I provided beforehand—would you have had any idea what *time* it was, *where* you were, *what* viewpoint you were supposed to assume, *what* the unknown viewpoint character did, *when* he opened the door (if indeed he did), *who* he saw standing *where*, *how* he felt, *why* he felt that way, *what* he did as a result, *where* the two of them went, *how* she was acting and *what* any of it meant?

The mistake of assuming reader knowledge of details in an imagined scene of this type is a very common one. Here the job facing the writer is fundamentally the same as that facing my student who needed to provide a great deal of evocative detail, letting the reader into the story world. But here the orientation work can and should be done much more briefly, in a word or two here and there, as the scene moves along at a fast pace.

As an exercise, let me urge you to take a few minutes out right now and write a brief expanded version of the four confusing lines I gave you above. What would you put in to tell me that it's Brad we start with, that he's home in his apartment, and that it's midnight? How do you say the doorbell sounded? (Hint: Often the simplest way to say something like this is just to *say it.*) Do you put in a sentence or clause showing him walking to the door? (I hope so.) Do you show him opening the door? (Again, I hope so.) Do you show Jill standing there, drab and disheveled, as he sees her, before either of them says anything? (I hope so!)

TAKING THINGS IN TURN

As you work on this exercise, realize that you still must be brief. But *steps cannot be left out.* So you must not only give me brief pointers as to who, where and when, but you must also give them to me *in the sequence in which they take place.* It would be deadly, for example, to skip from the sound of the doorbell to Brad's asking what's wrong. The reader will be disoriented with questions like, "Who's he talking to? Where? What is he seeing?" (Or, possibly, "How is he seeing her in the hall? The last thing I was told, he was sitting in the living room!"

Watch out, too, for habits in your grammar which might be perfectly correct, but confuse the reader's sense of sequence. For example, you should never write sentences that present story events out of their proper order, such as: "He offered her coffee after he had opened the door and invited her inside." This momentarily, at least, confuses the reader. Recast such sentences to put the opening of the door first, followed by other events in the order in which they took place.

Again, be aware that we'll enlarge on the concept of reader orientation several times later in this book, including the next two chapters. But the basic point is so important—and so frequently forgotten in first-draft writing of otherwise promising novels—that you should think seriously about it right here at the outset. *Keep the reader clearly oriented.*

PART TWO

Essential Techniques

Chapter Five

Viewpoint

E ons ago, long before the dawn of recorded history,
there was a caveman named Hrogthar.
Now, Hrogthar was what is commonly known as
a good old boy, but he was a nobody in his cave clan.
No one admired him or listened to him.

One day, walking through the jungle, Hrogthar was attacked
by a saber-toothed tiger. The tiger was huge and fearsome,
and all Hrogthar had for self-defense was his stone axe.

But Hrogthar was strong, and his terror gave him strength.
What a battle it was! The tiger scratched Hrogthar's arm.
Hrogthar whacked the tiger between the eyes with the axe.
The tiger staggered back through the forest and Hrogthar pur-
sued him. Then the tiger turned and counterattacked, and
drove Hrogthar to the brink of a great precipice over a river.
Hrogthar hit the tiger again. The tiger circled and nearly
backed Hrogthar over the precipice. Hrogthar narrowly
ducked a feint which would have exposed his breast to those
huge tiger fangs. Hrogthar swung his axe—and missed. The
tiger leaped. Hrogthar ducked. The tiger flew over his head—
and out into the empty space beyond the embankment.

The tiger plunged a thousand feet to the river below and
was carried away by the rampaging river.

That night, Hrogthar went back to the cave. Someone
around the campfire noticed the scratch on his arm.

"What happened to you?" asked a particularly beautiful
young maiden.

"I was walking in the woods today and a terrible tiger
attacked me," Hrogthar began—and he instantly noticed that
all voices hushed around the campfire, all eyes turned to him,

and for the first time in his life he was the center of attention.

So he told his story in vivid detail, leaving out nothing.

When Hrogthar finally finished his story, everyone applauded. The chief of the clan patted him on the back and gave him a choice mastodon steak to eat.

The next day, Hrogthar thought about all this.

Obviously, his telling of a story had gotten him fame and fortune.

He wanted more of both. But how? He let his imagination go to work.

That afternoon, Hrogthar intentionally cut his hand on a sharp rock. When he went home that night, he told a terrifying story of being attacked by a lion—and how the lion finally fell into quicksand and perished. (Which explained why there was no body for proof.)

Again everyone applauded and admired him, and the chief gave him a wonderful snake fillet for dinner.

"This is great," Hrogthar said to himself. And the next night he told his best story yet, about how he single-handedly bested a hairy mammoth, but of course could not drag the great beast back to the cave.

This time, however, something went wrong. The brave warriors turned away in disbelief that any single individual could have so many great adventures. And so that night Hrogthar went to bed hungry.

Hrogthar thought a lot about this, too. "I can't expect them to keep on believing indefinitely that every great exploit happened to me personally," he concluded. And he was very depressed.

Then, however, after many days of thought, he had an inspiration destined to change not only his life, but the world.

That night around the campfire he got everyone's attention and began, "Imagine, if you will, a lone warrior crossing the swamp. He is muddy and tired. *Imagine you are this warrior.* You know fierce animals are all around you, but you know you must press on. . . ."

A silence fell. Everyone listened, *willing to imagine they were the hero of the story so they would enjoy it.* They were captivated. So when Hrogthar finally finished the tale with a triumph for the warrior, all the listeners felt relieved after imagining such a grand adventure, the warriors applauded, and the chief gave Hrogthar first servings of the horsemeat stew.

What Hrogthar had invented was the most fundamental technique of storytelling: *placing the reader in the mind and heart of a person at the center of the story's action*—a foundation-stone approach we call viewpoint.

The reader wants to escape humdrum reality and have an adventure. If you, the writer, handle viewpoint correctly, the reader will identify with the central figure of the story—imaginatively become that viewpoint character and experience the story as she experiences her own life: from a limited field of knowledge and feeling, from one set of eyes, with all the uncertainty—and involvement—of actual experience.

Putting the viewpoint inside a character's head assures instant reader identification with that character. It's a technique so fundamental and universal that many writers tend to shrug off discussion of it because they think they know all about it. But errors in handling viewpoint are so common—and of so many different types—that more discussion is mandatory.

Today in fiction we sometimes see the point of view hopping all over the page within the confines of a single chapter or scene within a novel. That generally is not because the writer chose to do it, but because he came to us out of film, where the camera can hop all around, and doesn't know any better. Filmmakers don't have point of view. They have camera setups. They impose unity on their material through other devices.

But with the written word you have to be more careful than a filmmaker because credibility is harder won in print. When you're watching a movie, after all, you believe things more readily because *there the images are*, right in front of you on the screen, and it's hard to disbelieve what you're actually seeing with your own eyes. But the reader needs more help to identify and believe from the printed page. So viewpoint becomes enormously important.

RESTRICTION OF VIEWPOINT
We live our lives within a single viewpoint. We never get out of it—never really live in another person's head and heart. So if we are to make our fiction as lifelike as possible, shouldn't

we present the story from a single viewpoint, too, letting the reader experience the story just as he experiences real life?

Ordinarily, I think so. That's why, when students ask me if they can change viewpoint whenever they feel like it, I answer, "Yes, you can do that right after you get out of your own single, restricted viewpoint for one instant in real life."

The general rule, then, is this: Within a given chapter, or (at worst) within a given dramatic confrontation in your book, you *must* maintain the integrity of the viewpoint—and not switch.

Most beginning writers think this is a terrible imposition on their artistic freedom. Better writers gladly accept this seeming limitation as a useful control and focusing device, as well as an aid in building story credibility.

Can you ever change point of view? Of course. But you change when you decide to do so, for sound tactical reasons— not because you can, or vaguely feel like it, or have run out of gas in following a certain viewpoint character.

We'll elaborate on this later. But perhaps we have gotten ahead of ourselves, so let's fall back a few paces.

SELECTION OF THE VIEWPOINT CHARACTER

If you're going to accept limited viewpoint and write your novel almost entirely from a single viewpoint, how do you decide who that viewpoint character should be? The answer is that you pick the person:

- who will be at the center of the action;
- who will have everything at risk;
- whose struggle toward a goal is the fuel driving the story;
- who will be moved—changed—by the outcome.

Some of these observations run counter to the kind of permissiveness some scholars would suggest as acceptable. One such authority—William Flint Thrall and Addison Hibbard in their *A Handbook to Literature*, long out of print—says the viewpoint character can be someone remote from the action and only observing, and adds that the omniscient approach— author as god, being in everyone's head all the time—is a widespread technique.

Omniscience is often confusing, however, and is generally

out of favor in today's fiction. And the idea that the viewpoint can be a neutral observer is simply wrong.

In their *Theory of Literature*, Rene Wellek and Austin Warren suggest that a better name for viewpoint might be "focus of narration," since the viewpoint character is at the center of things. That definition is bothersome, however, since it doesn't seem quite personal enough. It might be helpful in picking the viewpoint character to remember "focus," however, because obviously you can't pick a viewpoint character who will be off at church while the central struggle takes place at the fairgrounds; your viewpoint person has to have a reason to be in all the right places at the right times—at the center of the action.

Also, the viewpoint character should be the person with everything at risk, to maintain reader interest and involvement. *Beware the neutral-observer viewpoint character!* The reader doesn't identify well with such folk, and mechanically such a viewpoint doesn't work for reasons we'll get to in a minute.

Notice the comment that the viewpoint character is the one whose goal motivation drives the story. Viewpoint characters, to be interesting, must be *active*! What happens in most popular fiction today is that the writer picks a person whose whole world is suddenly tilted out of kilter; that person (the viewpoint) struggles to make things right; the struggle is oriented toward a specific long-term goal, and the reader worries about it; and the outcome answers the fundamental question that the reader has been worried about—can the viewpoint character fight his way back to happiness?

In a story of *decision*, the viewpoint character is moved inexorably closer to some terrible moment of choice, a decision that finally will determine her ultimate happiness. And again the reader identifies with this viewpoint person and is carried along with the character's movement toward that all-important moment of final deciding.

In a story of *discovery*, again we have a central viewpoint character who is struggling against great odds to learn something being hidden, to come to terms with some inchoate problem that even she is not entirely sure of, to find some kind of peace with herself and the world. And here again the reader identifies, *cares*, and is carried along through the tale.

But whatever the story type, the viewpoint character cannot be passive and unconcerned. Successful viewpoint characters in modern fiction are never neutral or passive. They are active. They *try*. They are achievers—who do things.

As to the statement that the viewpoint character must be the moved character, fiction analyst Rust Hills pointed out long ago—as others had before him—that this is simply an inevitable dynamic of fiction, something inherent in the way good fiction has to work. In a story that works, the viewpoint character *will become* the moved character, or vice versa, even if the writer begins with a misconception about the matter.

Hills pointed out that in fiction, something happens to somebody. Someone is changed by the action. And that person who is most changed or moved is inevitably the viewpoint character.

Implied in Hills's discussion is the point that you should never even consider trying to write a novel about an observer character as the viewpoint. It's one of those things that sounds good, but never works.

Henry James learned this in writing his first novel, *Roderick Hudson*. James, later a consummate craftsman, had all kinds of trouble with this, his first novel. He tells us in a journal that he finally figured out why. He began with the title based on Hudson, but only very late in the revision did he finally realize that the story, despite its title, wasn't really about Roderick Hudson at all; it really was about the changes that took place in Mallett, the observer-viewpoint, as a result of his witnessing what took place in reference to Hudson.

Once James finally realized that Mallett, as the viewpoint character, *had to be* the central character because he was the one who was changed by the action, James could focus the book and revise it to make sense.

The same can be said about another misleadingly titled novel, *The Great Gatsby*. This novel hasn't translated well to film despite several attempts. One of the reasons is that the novel ultimately isn't about Jay Gatsby at all, but about Nick Carraway and what happens to *him* as a result of the action. At the end, Gatsby is dead and Tom and Daisy are going right on with their selfish, using little lives. They haven't changed. It is Carraway whose narrator tone changes as he describes the land as it used to be—and who decides at the end to return to the Midwest as a symbol of a purer lifestyle.

It's clear that F. Scott Fitzgerald finally understood this himself as he struggled with the novel. A few years ago I had a discussion with Budd Schulberg, a wonderful novelist and one-time associate of Fitzgerald. Schulberg had just finished going over all the drafts of Fitzgerald's *Gatsby*, comparing and analyzing.

One of the things that most struck Schulberg concerned the scene involving Carraway and his thoughts of the Indians and the earlier purity of the land. Up until the last revision, this scene took place very early in the novel, as an introduction to Carraway. Only after long labor did Fitzgerald realize that his story was Carraway's story after all, and Carraway could not have these feelings—be moved in this way—until after the climax of the action. It was only after Fitzgerald realized this— that Carraway's changed perception of the East was at the heart of the meaning of the book—that he moved the Indian scene all the way to the ending, where it gave focus to everything because it showed how the viewpoint character had been moved.

So, again, the viewpoint character—the person at the center—became the character moved by the action. It always works this way.

Do I seem to repeat myself? I hope so. It's one of the few things in all of life I am absolutely sure about. *There is no use trying to write a modern novel from the viewpoint of a passive observer. The dynamic of fiction will not let it work out that way.* So you might as well make your viewpoint character active at the center of the plot in the first place.

ESTABLISHING VIEWPOINT

How does one establish viewpoint?

First, you force yourself to imagine everything from inside the chosen viewpoint character.

Second, you use words, phrases and clauses which specify that the chosen viewpoint character is experiencing the story world through his senses, or having thoughts/feelings that only he could know.

If you follow the first precept, you'll never make the

mistake, for example, of getting into Harry's viewpoint and then telling the reader what Harry's facial expression looks like; unless Harry looks in a mirror, *he can't know what his expression looks like.* And you won't err by telling the reader what some other character is thinking or feeling, because Harry can't know that, either. The best he can do is guess. Which is, incidentally, the way we do it in real life.

Let's look at some examples.

The amateur writer of fiction will write "viewpointless" copy, like the following:

- Joe stood on the hill. Down below, a crowd was. . . .
- It was quiet. Then a sound. . . .
- Something crawled across Joe's hand. . . .
- Joe took a drink. It had almond flavoring. . . .
- Smoke filled the room. Joe got up. . . .

This is description or narration from no viewpoint. It's neutral. The reader doesn't know who he is supposed to be.

The professional writer imagines the events from inside the chosen viewpoint character. He will then reword his copy to prove that he is in that viewpoint, as follows:

- Looking down the hillside, *Joe could see.* . . .
- In the dark quiet, *Joe heard.* . . .
- *Joe felt* something crawl across his hand. . . .
- *Joe tasted* almond flavoring in the drink. . . .
- *Joe smelled* smoke and got up, *feeling panic.* . . .

REINFORCEMENT OF VIEWPOINT

The reader, once given such clear indications of where the viewpoint lies, will immediately "get into" the story and identify with the viewpoint character—and begin to experience the story in a very vivid way because he is experiencing the story as he experiences life, which is to say, from a single, restricted viewpoint.

But unfortunately readers tend to forget. Therefore, every few paragraphs, at least, the professional novelist will reinforce the viewpoint by making sure there are additional statements like those above. In addition, depending on the kind of story you happen to be telling, you may elect to give the reader more detailed, periodic reports of what the viewpoint character is thinking or feeling about the story action, other characters and his own plight. All this reinforces viewpoint and adds to reader enjoyment.

In my classes I have drills—copy analysis work—which prove that good writers constantly reinforce the point of view with statements of senses, feelings or thoughts in this way, and don't jump into some other viewpoint in the middle of the action except in very specialized cases, for very special reasons. (We'll look at some of those exotic situations later in this book, but for now it will be far better for your development if you pretend they don't even exist.)

A good self-test for you at this point might be to look at several pages of your own recent novel copy. Is it clear whose viewpoint you're in? Are you sure you haven't jumped into some other viewpoint without realizing it? Underline those words and phrases that identify or reinforce the viewpoint.

RESTRICTING VIEWPOINT OBSERVATIONS

Always keep uppermost in your mind the fact that you the writer should tell the reader *only* things the viewpoint character could know. Those are:

Sense impressions (seeing, hearing, feeling, tasting, smelling)
Thoughts
Emotions
Intentions

Consider: If you and I talk, there is no way for you to read my mind. Only I know what I'm thinking. Therefore, when you as a writer tell me directly and precisely what a character is thinking (without dialogue, of course), then you are at the same time establishing that character's viewpoint because *the only way we can know his thoughts is from his viewpoint.*

Emotions are exactly the same. If you write something like, "Janis felt fear and sadness like a winter chill," then I know I am in Janis's viewpoint because only Janis can definitely know what she is feeling. If you state a character's internal thoughts or intentions, the same is true. Only he can absolutely know them.

"But hold on!" I hear you say. "I often can look at a person and know exactly what he is feeling!" Nonsense. What you do when you see a woman weeping, for example, is observe the superficial clues and draw a conclusion about her emotional state. But you do not know what it is. You only guess.

And of course you can do the same in fiction. But you can't make your viewpoint character *know* another's thoughts or feelings.

Consider, for instance, a moment where our viewpoint, Joe, comes into a room and finds Anne weeping, then turning quickly away to hide her face from him. Let's make up two versions, the amateur first.

Amateur version:

> Joe walked into the room. Anne was standing on the other side, feeling very sad and crying, and Joe was curious, but when he stared at her she didn't want him to know how sad she really was so she turned away. Joe wondered what this was all about. Anne knew but kept it secret. Joe was confused.

Professional version, with key bits in capital letters:

> Walking into the room, *Joe saw* Anne weeping. *He felt pity* for her and *wondered* what was wrong. But Anne turned away quickly, and *Joe understood* that she didn't want him to see her tears, and *guessed* she must be trying to spare him. Still, as *he watched her* tremble, *he felt* confused.

In viewpoint a character can experience his own internal processes, and observe and make guesses about the outside world. No more.

HANDLING "NON-VIEWPOINT" SEGMENTS

Of course everything you write in a given section of your novel will not be studded exclusively with "he saw" or "she felt" segments. You may subtly shift away from such sentence constructions to tell in a rather netural tone how your viewpoint character drove downtown, for example, or how certain past events may have contributed to the present action. Such descriptions or statements about the story action are an integral part of your storytelling. There is no reason for you to worry if you encounter these in your copy as long as you don't use a verbal construction in them that forces the reader into some other viewpoint. As mentioned earlier, the reader, once in a viewpoint, will tend to assume she is *still* in that viewpoint until you do something to force her to conclude otherwise.

Thus it is that most novelists can establish a viewpoint, then "get away with" some straight narration or exposition that isn't literally in the viewpoint of the chosen character, but is accepted by the reader anyway.

Even in such "non-viewpoint" passages, however, it can help your reader's sense of involvement if you can make sure that nothing in your chosen language or assumed attitude might be foreign to the viewpoint character. It could be disastrous, for example, to be in the viewpoint of an illiterate child, then slide into a bit of narration or exposition in which you use big, specialized words, or express deep insights about human behavior that your viewpoint character (always standing nearby, remember!) simply could not know.

To put this in a more positive light, even your "non-viewpoint" or neutral transitional passages will be more convincing if you can contrive ways to make them "sound" true to your viewpoint character.

An excellent example of this is in the work of crime writer Elmore Leonard. He is widely recognized as a master of contemporary dialogue in fiction. Less often remarked is his uncanny ability to put transitional material—almost "author copy"—into the intelligence level, attitude, vocabulary, emotion, thinking cadence and total evident personality of the last-seen viewpoint character.

The technique Leonard uses for this is very, very advanced, and beyond our scope here. However, to get a clearer view of this kind of "non-viewpoint" writing, you may want to get a copy of his novel *Rum Punch*. In the bibliography I've cited the paperback edition so you can buy a copy and perhaps mark it up a bit.

You don't have to read far to see Leonard's extraordinary facility with viewpoint at work. Read chapter three. Here we have been in the viewpoint of a clever, lawless, street-smart African-American criminal named Ordell; although much of the brief chapter contains *no* statements to establish viewpoint directly, and is largely background information that could have been written in neutral language, everything is worded and phrased in Ordell's pacing and vocabulary.

Having studied this chapter, turn to the next one. The viewpoint is different. Here, too, however, we are quickly moved into "author narration" that gives neutral background and information. But the language, pacing, tone and feel of the copy here are *entirely different*—again true to the last-identified viewpoint character.

You don't have to become as expert as Elmore Leonard to handle those parts of your book where you slip in needed information or transitional material. But if you take the time to study a master at the game, you will get valuable additional insights into how vital viewpoint really is in terms of credibility and reader involvement.

THE "TEMPERATURE" OF VIEWPOINT PRESENTATION

Obviously, every writer has her individual style and method of presenting the viewpoint in a story.

In a romance novel, for example, the viewpoint is usually very "warm"—with many excursions deep into the protagonist's most intense and personal feelings, long descriptions of how she feels and how she experiences tactile sensations, analysis of her thoughts and intentions, and a style that sometimes is intense, heavily colored by highly connotative words, and so on.

In a spy novel, on the other hand, the viewpoint may be very "cool," or even cold. We may be told very little about what the character is thinking, and virtually nothing about what the character may be feeling. The effect may approach an appearance of objectivity.

How you handle your rendition of viewpoint will depend to some degree on your own tendencies as a writer, but more so—I hope—on the kind of story you are telling and the dramatic effects you want to achieve. James Bond would never lapse into emphatic soul-searching like the heroines of some romance novels. But a heroine in a romance would not "work" as a character if she were super-cool like 007, either.

Whether the viewpoint is hot or cold, warm or cool, will also tend to depend on story circumstance. It's absurd to have your male viewpoint experience intense emotional reactions (which you describe in detail), be aware of every physical sensation with great intensity, and be thinking in an agony of clear perception and uncertainty if he is sitting safe and snug in his warm mountain cabin, toasting his toes before the fire. But if you put the same male character on the side of the mountain, beside a stalled car, with his dying child stuck inside the car during a blizzard—her life depending on his solution to their terrible problem—then that same male viewpoint might very well be presented in tones and depths infinitely warmer than you would have otherwise used.

The more pressing the story circumstances, the warmer the viewpoint will tend to be. That's inevitable. But you may, for reasons of irony or mystery, choose to keep the viewpoint cool even in a time of crisis. That's up to you. The point is that viewpoint temperature changes. You control it. Know your temperature, and why it is as it is.

The tendency today generally is for the author to imagine the scene from a very hot, totally involved viewpoint. The first draft may even be written this way, because it's always easier to cool a scene down later than it is to warm one up. But most fiction today is presented in its final form from a fairly cool point of view—a moderately detached authorial position.

The general advice, then, would seem to be: *Imagine it hot. Revise it cool.*

ANALYTICAL ASSIGNMENT

At this point, I feel sure, you are confident you understand exactly how viewpoint works. But it never hurts to ground understanding with work. Further, one of the lifetime tools I hope you will take from this book is the habit of analyzing published copy, as well as your own, in order to learn new things about the craft. Therefore, I hope you will take the time at this point to do a little "lab work" for me—but really for yourself.

Take a contemporary novel. Pick one chapter. Go through it and underline in RED every word that absolutely specifies the viewpoint with a phrase such as "she thought," "he heard," or whatever. Then, with BLUE, underline all those portions which you *assume* are in the same viewpoint, even if there is no specific viewpoint pointer in that sentence, paragraph or subsection. If you spot a place where the viewpoint character speculates about another's internal processes or draws conclusions from the evidence about same, bracket those in GREEN. Put an ORANGE X in the margin every time viewpoint is reinforced with another direct statement such as "She saw." Circle "warm" adjectives and adverbs with PURPLE.

Go back to the Elmore Leonard novel mentioned earlier and mark up at least one more chapter in a similar way.

Look at what you've done. Can you draw any conclusions? *Force yourself to write down at least six conclusions* that can be drawn from your analysis. Put these in your journal. Ask yourself—and answer—such questions as the following:

1. How many ways does this author establish viewpoint? (Thought, sense impressions, emotion, intention.)
2. How often does this author reinforce the viewpoint?
3. How many different word combinations are used to reinforce viewpoint? List them.
4. Does the writer "hit" all the senses?
5. Does the writer have her character do more feeling or more thinking? Why?
6. Is this viewpoint warm or cool? Why?

This is only a suggestive list. The more questions you can think of to ask when you analyze, the more you will learn. Good writers never stop analyzing and learning.

I wish I could face you as you read these words, and give you a shake for emphasis. Analysis is a key part of your learner's permit. If you fail to do some of the analyses and exercises suggested here—or do them halfheartedly, without forcing yourself to think just as hard as you can about them—you're cheating yourself out of growth.

VIEWPOINT MAKES EVERY CHARACTER UNIQUE

The vital technique of viewpoint is something you can never learn too much about. Your handling of it is what will make your story—no matter how familiar the plot—fresh and unique.

Why? Because each of us lives in a unique universe. As we'll discuss in chapters twelve and thirteen, good characters seem real; they are, in addition, driven by dedication to personal ideals and even symbols. Our primary motivation isn't self-preservation, some authorities suggest, but preservation of the *symbolic self.* Each of us builds our life around an idea of ourself, and we do everything to preserve that self-concept. Even the stimuli we choose to notice are based on our unique idea of self.

If you and I were to take a walk through a shopping mall, we would not experience the same place. You might notice a clothing store, a candy shop and the children playing around the fountain. I, on the other hand, might notice the electronic gadgets at Radio Shack, the health foods store display or a new pipe at the pipe shop.

Further, if you were depressed and I was feeling good, you would experience the mall as rather dusty, loud and perhaps dreary, while I would notice the sunshine coming through the skylights, and how it glinted on a girder.

In real life, as in fiction, we reach out to the environment and pluck out from a million stimuli those that fit our idea of ourself and our mood. That's why the viewpoint in your fiction will decide *everything* about the story world. Viewpoint is the lens through which everything is seen.

A WRITING EXERCISE

Now take the time to run a quick check on your own handling of viewpoint, as well as your tendencies in handling it.

Next, read the brief "situation" exercise that follows, then take ten minutes (no more) and write about this moment I have given you twice, as directed.

After you have done this work—*and not until then*—read past the given excerise to a brief section where you will be asked some questions to help you analyze the work you have done in terms of your understanding of viewpoint and your own tendencies in writing viewpoint.

SITUATION: A cold and lonely morning, with windy, cloudy gray sky. High cliffs overlooking the stormy sea. A man stands on the cliff top, facing the sea, his back to the rocky path and meadow behind and below him. The man wears a heavy blue coat and hat. He appears grim. Behind him, a young woman runs across the wet, icy meadow. She wears only a thin summer dress and light sandals. She is bare-legged and has no coat. She runs up the rocky path. When she is only a step behind the man, he turns to face her.

YOUR INSTRUCTIONS: Write this sequence of events *twice.*

FIRST, from the man's viewpoint.

SECOND, from the woman's viewpoint.

Take no more than ten minutes for each.

Do not feel you have to go earlier in time to establish this moment, or to follow it into later action. Simply write this bit of business twice, once as if the man were the viewpoint character, then again as if the woman were the viewpoint character.

Don't read on until you have done this work!

ANALYSIS OF YOUR OWN WORK

Some questions to ask yourself about the man's viewpoint exercise:

1. Did the man see his grim facial expression? I hope not. He can't see his own face.

2. Did he see the girl coming up behind him? How? I didn't tell you he turned. In the man's sequence, the girl cannot be seen until she speaks to him or makes a noise, causing him to turn. (Nobody has eyes in the back of his head.)

3. Did the man feel the cold wind? Sea spray? Did he smell the sea? I hope he had some of these very strong sense impressions.

4. Did the man have some thought processes going on? Did you by any chance make up an intention for him?

Questions about the woman's viewpoint:

1. Was she cold? Did you say so? Certainly, above all else, she would experience cold, dressed as she is. Did you tell us so?

2. Bare legs. Wet grass in a meadow. Very cold and uncom-

fortable. Did you mention the wet grass on the bare legs? Isn't that pretty important as a viewpoint-defining sense impression?

3. Did you have her thinking anything? Having an intention? *Because she is the active one here*, it is much more important that you give *her* some thought, and an intention, than it was in the male exercise. (He was just standing, looking grim. But she must have a reason for running out in the cold to find him!)

4. Did her sense impressions change any as she neared the top of the cliffs—did she feel more wind, hear the sea, get colder? I hope so.

5. You didn't make the mistake of telling us what her face looked like, did you? There's no mirror—in her viewpoint she can't see her face!

Incidental question about both excerpts: Did you write the exercises in first or third person? You can do either, you know.

Finally, here's another suggestion as an added learning bonus:

To get a handle on your tendencies as a writer of viewpoint, go back through each exercise again with some colored pencils at hand. Mark each physical sense impression in RED. Mark each thought in BLUE. Mark each statement of emotion in GREEN. Mark each statement of intention in BLACK.

I hope you will find a nice mixture of colors, which would indicate that you are using all your viewpoint-identifying tools. If you notice one color missing entirely after your markup, or a tremendous predominance of one, it might mean something about your copy generally.

- No RED could mean an abstract reading experience that the reader probably could never get into imaginatively, and experience vicariously with her own senses.
- No BLUE would mean a story filled with characters who run around meaninglessly, as far as the reader is concerned, because it's through a viewpoint character's thoughts that we understand what the story is all about.
- No GREEN could mean robots, not people—a cold story, and no reader would care.
- No BLACK could mean, ultimately, no plot.

Think about what the balance of colors in your viewpoint exercise means. If you realize that your tendency has been to leave something out, then make a note to be aware of this shortcoming in your writing. Again, put some notations in your work journal. Set up a practice writing schedule and analyze your copy some more at later times. Analyze more published novel passages for new ideas. Practice and analysis will lead to improvement.

LOOKING AHEAD

We'll return to the subject of viewpoint at other spots in this book, especially in chapter nine when we consider scene structure. In the meantime, the creative and analytical work suggested here should keep you from dashing immediately into chapter six. Remember what was said earlier about providing a little "soak time." Do the work. Then take a day off from this book and learning more new stuff. Do your three- or five- or ten-page quota, and come back here fresh.

And if you run out of things to do, remember an earlier thought about meditation and the creative wellsprings. Sit back for a few minutes, close your eyes, and think about a mountain or a lake or a flower.

Or even that other beautiful thing in your life—your novel.

Chapter Six

Stimulus and Response

You happen to meet a friend on the street.
She says, "Hello."
You say, "Hello."

You're heating water for coffee, and burn yourself.
You jerk back from the pain.

The telephone rings.
You answer it.

The doctor taps your knee with his little hammer.
Your leg jerks.

Simple transactions like this happen all the time. They illustrate the basic principle of *stimulus and response*, a mechanism governing an astonishing number of everyday events.

It's also the mechanism that can make your fiction make sense and move forward in a disciplined line that will enthrall your reader.

The bottom-line rule: For every stimulus, there is a response. Or, conversely, for every response, there must be a stimulus.

Seeing how straightforward the pattern is, one wonders why so much fiction is screwed up in terms of stimulus and response, making it unpublishable.

Maybe it's because many writers don't like to believe that humans are really so mechanistic and predictable. The idea of a knee-jerk existence is repulsive to most of us. But money-making writers believe in the principle for ordering their fiction, whether or not they accept the theories of psychologists like B.F. Skinner in real life. Fiction has to be *bigger than life* in many ways, and this is one of them.

Enlarging on the bottom-line rule just a bit to apply it to your novel: Whenever you show something happening (a stimulus), you must show something else happening as a result (a response); and whenever you desire a certain thing to happen (a response), you must show the happening that caused it (the stimulus).

If you show a stimulus but fail to show a response to it, the stimulus becomes meaningless because it didn't make anything happen. Do this very often and readers lose interest in your book because nothing seems significant. If you show something happening (a response) without providing a cause for it (a stimulus), your transaction won't make sense and your reader will quit you out of confusion and/or disbelief.

But follow the simple basic pattern and you will begin to write copy that not only makes good sense, but steams along like a locomotive. In our eclectic approach to writing, I won't often mention behavioristic ideas. But for this aspect of work, you need to accept it 100 percent.

Stimulus and response works whether you are trying to get someone to duck his head (you throw something at him!) or plan his next step in a complicated plot. It works in dialogue and dramatic action, and it works in planning the architecture of your book. Sometimes it's very simple; other times just a bit more complicated. But in any case, you can learn to handle it routinely.

THE SIMPLE TRANSACTION

The simple transaction is almost like the knee-jerk reaction. Someone calls your name and you turn your head. Thunder crashes and you jump. "Duck!" someone yells, and you duck. Or—

"Will you marry me, Cindy?" he asked.
"Yes, oh, yes!" Cindy sighed.

So when the response seems straightforward and easily understood, all you have to do as a writer is make sure both the stimulus and response are presented:

- clearly,
- in the proper order,
- with nothing skipped, and
- close together, so the relationship is not obscured.

Which sounds absurdly easy, but can get messed up if you
don't watch out.

Consider this transaction:

> Joe walked to the door and opened it.
> "I was wondering if you were home."

Seeing this, the reader is confused. "Why did Joe walk to
the door? Who's talking in the second paragraph?" he asks.
"Who is *whoever* talking to? What's going on here?"

Clearly some kind of stimulus-response relationship is suggested by the close juxtapositioning of Joe walking to the door
and someone starting to talk. But clearly something is wrong.

You ask the author about it.

"Oh!" he says. "Well, first thing, Joe heard the doorbell
ring (stimulus), so he went to the door and opened it (response), and then he saw Archibald standing there (stimulus)
and he said, 'What are you doing here?' (his response, which
becomes a stimulus to Archibald), so Archibald said, 'I was
wondering if you were home.' "

Oh. Well, fine. But it wasn't written very clearly in the first
place, was it?

"I guess," the author says lamely, "I need to pay more
attention."

Yes. Assumptions by the author that he forgets to put in the
stimulus-and-response (S&R) presentation itself are a prime
cause of confusion and obscurity in such transactions. Stimulus
and response provide clarity, logic and movement—but not if
you assume things in your head and forget to put them down
on the paper.

Putting stimulus and response down *in the wrong order* is an
even more common cause of confusion. Consider:

> Bob hit the dirt, hearing the explosion.

Anything wrong with that?

Grammatically, no. Tactically, in terms of good fiction,

everything.

The structure of the sentence reversed the order of stimulus and response. Reading such a sentence, for just an instant, the reader is disoriented. The explosion is the stimulus. It has to come first. Then the response, Bob's hitting the dirt.

This seems like a small matter. But if you string dozens of similar order-reversal sentences into your novel, the reader will get uneasy, maybe confused, and ultimately disgusted.

So the sentence above should be recast:

> Hearing the explosion, Bob hit the dirt.
> *or*—
> Something exploded. Bob hit the dirt.

Or some other variation that puts stimulus and response in the correct order.

This may seem absurdly elementary, but in the white heat of composition, some very good writers have been known to forget it. Please don't assume you're perfect. Look at your own copy and make sure you are not leaving out the stimulus, assuming something the reader can't possibly know from reading your page or writing in such a style that the stimulus hits the reader's consciousness after the response.

You'll find, incidentally, that writing good S&R copy may have a subtle impact on your writing style. You'll tend to write shorter grammatical units. You will seldom—unless you *intend* to convey confusion—use constructions like "while," "as he . . .," and "at the same time as . . .," because these connote *simultaneity*, and in good S&R writing that just doesn't happen: You show the cause, then you show the effect.

Although the example above about Joe walking to the door was an example of simple confusion-through-omission, there can be even more serious ones, leading to worse complications for the reader. Consider this excerpt:

> Susan collected her mail and went inside her house, screaming and crying.

QUERY TO THE AUTHOR: *"Hey, this doesn't make sense."*

AUTHOR: *"Oh! I forgot to put in there that she opened a letter and read that her mother and father just died."* Long *pause, then . . . thoughtfully: "I guess maybe I should have put that in?"*

Don't skip! Readers can't provide what you left out, and the entire S&R pattern is wrecked.

A similar problem can arise from excessive separation between stimulus and response. Imagine, if you will, a wife hurling a lamp at her husband and konking him on the noggin. Then the author gives us a long scene between the wife and her mother on the phone, a talk with a lawyer and a description of the sunset. And then, fifteen pages later, we come to the husband bandaging his head.

Chances are in many such cases the reader will have forgotten what stimulated the husband to need a bandage, and the whole thing will be very puzzling, at least momentarily. S&R packages need to fit closely in story time and page space.

It might be a good idea for you to stop right now and check some of your own copy for simple stimulus and response errors!

THE COMPLICATED TRANSACTION

All S&R transactions, you will note, are not as conveniently simple as those we've dealt with so far.

What if, for example, we return to the marriage proposal we used earlier and change the response a bit?

> "Will you marry me, Cindy?" he asked.
> Cindy burst into tears and slapped his face.

Or, instead of having someone touch a hot stove and jerk back in reflex, what if we have two men facing each other across a restaurant table, and one of them extends his hand, putting it in the flame of the table candle, and then, instead of jerking back, *he leaves his hand in the flame, cooking?*

Obviously, something more complicated is happening at such times. Every S&R transaction is not as simple as a knee jerk.

Underlying this is the fact that in every transaction, no matter how simple and straightforward, there is always a step—often hidden—between the stimulus and the response; this process of *internalization* takes place inside the mind, heart and body of the person receiving the stimulus and preparing a response.

When we're writing an uncomplicated transaction, we don't need to show the internalization. In the case of "Hello"— "Hello" or the jerking of your knee when tapped with the rubber mallet, it's machine-like and predictable. But when Cindy bursts into tears or the man feels the candle pain and ignores it, something more is going on, and we as writers have to provide the internalization so the reader will understand the response—and the meaning of the transaction.

To paraphrase that because it's so important: *When the S&R transaction is complicated, you may have to "play" the internalization—write it down for the reader—so the reader will understand the response.*

So we might fix Cindy this way:

> (*Stimulus*) "Will you marry me, Cindy?" he asked.
> (*Internalization*) The question shocked her. How could he ask, right after she had seen him in the bedroom with Sue? Rage flooded through her and
> (*Response*) She burst into tears and slapped his face.

Now the transaction makes some kind of sense.

This is the way more complex S&R transactions must be presented if they are to make immediate sense to the reader. The pattern is:

1. Stimulus (external event) which causes:
2. Internalization (thought and/or emotion inside the view-point character) which explains and leads directly to:
3. Response (external event).

I leave it to you to write an internalization for the man holding his hand in the cafe candle. It might just be that he'll feel the agonizing pain but remember that he must prove to his colleague that he is fanatically tough and self-disciplined, so he fights the pain, fights the impulse to jerk his hand out of the flame, and sits there with his own flesh cooking.

(If that sounds farfetched, perhaps you aren't old enough to remember one of the weirder players in the Watergate scandal and some of the autobiographical posturing that later came from him.)

INTERNALIZATION EQUALS QUICKIE CHARACTERIZATION

Understanding and acceptance of the internalization principle, incidentally, leads to the answer to a question frequently asked by beginning novelists: "When do I go inside the character's head?" One part of the answer: When you must, to explain a complicated and unexpected response to a stimulus.

So if you want to drop in a bit about the character's thinking or feeling process, or even a tiny bit of background, you simply provide a complicated stimulus, and the character is forced to pause an instant and react internally in order to formulate the unexpected response.

PUZZLING THE READER ON PURPOSE

There may be times, of course, especially in mystery fiction, when the experienced craftsman will purposely leave out internalization in order to create a puzzling transaction—in order to heighten reader tension and curiosity. That's a somewhat advanced technique. Done well, it can be fascinating now and then. Done awkwardly, it's only confusing. If you're new to the idea of stimulus and response in writing your fiction, I urge you to handle such transactions very straightforwardly for a while, until you absolutely have it down pat. Only then can you risk tinkering with the norm in an attempt to achieve a desired special effect. It's far safer most of the time to resist the impulse to be cute, and instead adhere to the general rule: When the transaction is complex, you should "play" the internalization in order for the reader to understand the response.

BACKGROUND MOTIVATION IS NOT STIMULUS

Also, please give this some additional thought, in case you did not fully appreciate the implications in what's gone before: Stimulus is external, specific and immediate. And background is not stimulus.

For example, if Carolyn goes to her medicine cabinet to take two aspirin, and I ask you why she did this, in terms of stimulus and response, *don't*, please, say something like, "She just happened to think about it." That's inside her (an internalization, of course) and I'll just be a jerk and demand, "What was the *stimulus*, then, for that thought to occur?"

Such inadvertent begging of the question—mistaking something internal for a stimulus, which must be *external* to the viewpoint character—is a very common and troublesome error.

Similarly, you can't explain the trip for aspirin by saying Carolyn had had a headache for two days. To work right, a stimulus must be specific and immediate. The fact that Carolyn had had a headache for a long time is not good enough—it's *background information.* The reader, at some mysterious level, will not believe the transaction. It's all well and good to let me know that the headache had persisted all day, but my question as a reader is, "Why didn't she take aspirin earlier? At noon? Five minutes ago? Or why didn't she wait another five minutes? Why right this instant?"

To make it work, you have to show a transaction like this:

> Carolyn's headache pulsed, as it had all day. *(Background)*
> Thunder blasted outside. *(Stimulus)*
> Her head pulsed more painfully. *(Internalization)*
> She got up and went to the bathroom. . . . *(Response)*

Now we see the logicality and immediate-cause relationship between the thunder and the aspirin tablets.

In writing workshops I sometimes pass out a sheet listing a number of actions. The task is to provide a stimulus for what's presented, and then provide a response to what's given.

One of them reads like this:

> Sam dropped the lighted cigarette into the gasoline.

What would be the immediate stimulus for this?

Not something like "Sam wanted to blow something up," "Sam had been angry at the gas station owner for days" or "Sam didn't know fire would ignite gasoline."

All that stuff is background.

Rather, it must be something like the following:

> "Drop that cigarette, fool!" *or*
> The cigarette burned Sam's fingers *or*
> A car backfired, making Sam jump.

See the point? Immediate and specific and external—and

not old background motivation which might have caused the action any old time.

TAILORING THE RESPONSE

But suppose you have the cigarette already falling toward the puddle of gasoline. What *response* do you put in next?

Before reading another word here, take out a sheet of scratch paper and complete the transaction.

Stimulus: The cigarette falls into the gasoline.
Response: ? (You write it down.)

♦ ♦ ♦

Done? Fine. Now please don't tell me you wrote something like any of the following:

The fire trucks came. *(This skips steps in the chain of stimulus-response events, right?)*

Sam was horrified. *(Skip! Nothing has happened yet to horrify him. You have to show the result of the cigarette hitting the gasoline next, so that it can, in turn, become a new external stimulus to Sam.)*

(Of course, if you have him realize what he has done and be horrified as the cigarette falls, fine. But you're just adding another internalization step in the stimulus package and you still have to show the result of the cigarette hitting the gasoline. See discussion below.)

The owner raced out of the station. *(Why? Would he do this before something else happens with the gasoline?)*

Oh dear, Sam thought. *(Nothing has happened yet. How can he be thinking this? To what external stimulus is this the internalization?)*

No, the response to Sam's dropping of the cigarette into the gasoline almost has to be some variation of an orange flash, an explosion, flames sizzling across the tarmac or something of that nature. Fire trucks may come, Sam may be horrified, etc., etc. But the *first thing* that happens must result from the cigarette hitting the gasoline.

Also, please notice that Sam's horror—even if it takes place as he realizes what he has done before the cigarette hits the pavement—should not be presented to the reader *in that order* because to do so would place too much verbiage between the outside stimulus and the outside response. I mean, the next thing that's going to happen is a hell of a fire. That—not Sam's horror—will be the immediate response to the falling cigarette. Putting horror in there only separates stimulus and response, confusing the issue.

We'll talk more about the order of presentation in S&R packages when we get into dialogue in chapter fourteen. The broader issue underlying the principle, that of cause and effect generally, gets close scrutiny and discussion in chapters nine and sixteen. Here, however, one additional point must be made to avoid confusion.

KEEP S&R TRANSACTIONS STRAIGHTFORWARD

Most of us have witnessed world-class tennis at some time or other, watching as a great player blasted a forehand, saw the opponent's return going crosscourt, raced over to hit a backhand, sensed his opponent in retreat and rushed to the net to hit a winning volley.

Great stuff. Pure stimulus and response, possibly with a little internalization-anticipation thrown in. But even that great player we just watched would have been reduced to utter confusion if, instead of seeing one ball come across the net, he had been forced to try to react to six!

If it's so simple to see in tennis, shouldn't it be as clear in writing? The rule:

one stimulus = one response.

Look at this little bit of action:

> Ralph exploded into the room. He threw his wrench at Ted. He yelled, "I'm going to kill you, Ted!" He raced across the room and hit Ted with a haymaker. "Are you going to confess or not?" he screamed.

Now you tell me what Ted's response is going to be!

It's at times like this that writers often lean back from the keyboard and say, "Geez, I'm stuck!"

Why?

It's obvious. Too many stimuli. We ganged up on poor Ted

and bombarded him with several tennis balls, not giving him time to react to them in turn. So now that we've finally decided to give the poor guy a response, we're as confused as he is, trying to figure out what he'll respond to.

So maybe we make a desperation try at a response like this:

> Ted ducked the wrench. "Why do you want to kill me?" he replied. He reeled back from the force of the blow. "Never!"

And of course that doesn't make sense either!

Get it? To have clear S&R transactions, make it a habit to send one ball over the net at a time. Have it hit back. Hit another ball. Take things logically, one step at a time.

And each time you conclude a stimulus, ordinarily, hit the return key. *Make a new paragraph.* The stimulus goes in one paragraph, the response in the next one. That helps with clarity, too.

And if you *must* have Ralph send more than one stimulus at a whack, please remember these points:

1. All parts of one stimulus package go in the same paragraph. When the stimulus package ends, the paragraph ends.
2. If more than one stimulus is sent, *the responder will always react to the last stimulus sent.*

Here's an example.

Suppose Bill feels sorry for something he has done, goes to Ronald, says he's sorry and offers to shake hands.

You *cannot* write it this way:

> "I'm sorry, Ronald," Bill said, holding out his hand. He felt sorry.

Why is this impossible? Because the last thing you've put in the paragraph is internalization, and Ronald cannot conceivably respond to that. So if internalization is involved, it can't go last in the paragraph.

You *can*, however, write it two other ways:

> Bill felt sorry. He held out his hand. "I'm sorry, Ronald." Now Ronald speaks.

or—
Bill felt sorry. "I'm sorry, Ronald," he said, holding out
his hand.   Ronald ignores his gesture, miffed .

Which will you choose? The answer depends on which stimulus in the package you want Ronald to respond to. If you
want Ronald to speak, you put Bill's words last. But if you
want Ronald to dash Bill's hand aside or stare contemptuously
at it, you'll put the hand last.

IT TAKES PRACTICE
Consider, analyze and practice your own S&R presentations.
Don't assume they're okay—because if you haven't put in a
lot of hard work honing your skill in this area, they probably
aren't!

As at the end of earlier chapters, give yourself a break—a
learning break. Take some of your own copy and mark it up,
putting stimulus and response markers in the margins and noting whether you are following the rules. Do you find internalizations? Are they where they should be? Have you inadvertently skipped some steps in a chain of S&R transactions?

Take your time. The work may make all the difference
between clear, dramatic copy—and a mess. After doing some
of your analysis, log your results in your journal. Make a note
to analyze your own copy again six months from now.

No rush. If you devote a week or two to working on the
techniques of stimulus and response—even to devising practice transactions for yourself to write in your journal—it will
be time well spent. In semester-long classes I devote two
weeks—six or seven class hours—to this topic alone. It's that
important.

Chapter Seven

Goal Motivation
and the Story Question

Your reader wants to enjoy your story. In order to enjoy the story, she has to know *what to worry about.*

How do you tell her what to worry about? You make it perfectly clear that your lead viewpoint character wants something—something specific, identifiable, possibly attainable (against great odds)—that's vital to his happiness.

You can tell the reader that your lead character wants almost anything, as long as the character defines the goal as vital. The reader will immediately take the goal statement and turn it around into *a story question*—and worry about it.

Like the goal statement, this question is never vague. Examples:

You write: Andrea wanted to get a job in the ballet.
The reader worries: Will Andrea get a job in the ballet?

You write: "I've got to get to Akron," Bill said.
The reader worries: Can Bill get to Akron?

You write: Darlene knew it was vital to win the election.
The reader worries: Will Darlene win the election?

Note, please, that these statements of goal are all positive, rather than negative. It's much easier to write about positive goals.

THE VALUES OF POSITIVE MOTIVATION
You can, of course, write about negative motivations. Like Rita, who wants to prevent Barney from getting the jewels. And a lot of great books have been written from such negative motivations. But when you start with your lead character

operating in a preventive configuration, it usually means that the antagonist is already into a positive, goal-motivated game plan. And that often means that your lead character has already, in the conception, been shoved into a negative, *reacting*, rather than acting, role. And that's just not good. You've put your presumably main character in a secondary role in terms of making the plot go.

Of course your lead character will encounter many setbacks, disasters and surprises, and will often be forced into a role of reacting in the playing out of the story conflict. It's hard enough to keep her active, and not always just tossing up defensive lobs, when you start her out with a positive game plan. When you start her out negatively, she often gets pushed into reeling from pillar to post, trying to stop things, and never gets to initiate much on her own—which tends to make her look wimpy or poorly motivated.

As we'll see in chapter nine, the viewpoint character's goal not only fuels the story, but holds every dramatic segment together. Therefore it's vital to state your lead character story goal in positive terms as often as possible.

And it's almost always possible.

Good thing. Most of us admire people who initiate things rather than those who are always saying, "No, no, not that!" The legislator fighting for a new law he authored may be admirable to us even if we aren't crazy about the law. The legislator who is always yelling nay and staging filibusters quickly loses our sympathy.

Maybe it's nearly universal to admire someone trying to get something done rather than someone fighting a rearguard holding action.

MAKING THE GOAL SPECIFIC

Something else to note: Even though the goal statements given in the examples above are quite broad enough to become the backbone of an entire novel, they are all based on a specific desire. The reader can't worry very pleasurably if your goal statement is something like "Joe wanted to be happy" or "Marie wanted to do something about her problems."

Sometimes when I tell a class this I detect a murmur of protest from some corner of the room. I call on the protester, and he invariably says something like, "But *in real life* people often drift along without a specific goal!"

And I reply, "Yes, but we aren't talking about real life here. We're talking about a simulation of life that's better."

At which point sometimes I get a drop slip because there will always be those who can't see that art improves on life, and exists because it does so.

Ah, well.

THE ANSWER SHOULD BE "YES" OR "NO"

Another item to note: The reader's formulation of the story goal into a story question is always a question that can be answered Yes or No. The story question grows out of a goal statement that says somebody wants something, and the question always is "Will he get it?" "Can he do it?" "Does she succeed?" A clear, simple question—and the source of all curiosity and suspense in everything that follows.

In a novel, the lead character's long-term goal thus forms the major story question—the umbrella question that hangs over the entire book. And ultimately the reader reads to get the answer. Many secondary questions may arise as the novel moves along, many steps forward and steps back. But the umbrella question remains, and the relevance of everything you put in your novel depends somehow on its relationship to that umbrella story question—even if the remote connection exists only in your viewpoint's mind.

Look at virtually any "formed" novel you ever enjoyed— one you read with great tension and curiosity and suspense. From virtually the first page you knew what the long-term goal was, and you had your story question. Often it was made perfectly explicit in the text itself. Sometimes you guessed it from the context and hints the author gave you. But you knew what you were worrying about.

Even in the harder-to-write novel of discovery or decision, the viewpoint character should clearly know that she wants to discover *something*, or decide about *something*, even if she isn't entirely sure at the outset what that might turn out to be. In this sense, every good novel is a novel involving a quest.

Do you want to start your book in a way that makes sense and will involve the reader? Then establish your lead character and let her tell another character—or allow yourself to speak for her—precisely what she wants and why it's vital to her. The reader will turn it into a story question, and start reading with interest.

OBSTACLES ARE ESSENTIAL

Of course you need more than a good start to keep the story going. It's all well and good to set up a character and a goal— but if the character gets the goal too soon or too easily, your book dies. The key to maintaining reader tension and interest is to delay the climax *by putting obstacles between the character and attainment of the goal.*

How do you do that? By now I hope you sense the answer. You do it by setting up another character who has a vested interest in reaching the lead's goal before she does, or in thwarting the lead's quest. In other words, you introduce that vital story element we discussed in chapter three: conflict.

Antag.

As I said, every good novel at some level is the record of a quest. For a quest to have continuing interest, you need not only adversity, but conflict, standing between the lead viewpoint character and the goal.

In a writing career spanning decades, I have had three serious slumps—times when the ideas simply would not come, and everything I wrote felt stale and insipid. On one of those occasions, I sensed that my imagination had grown weary of developing story material by interposing conflictful obstacles between my viewpoint and the goal. Making up and developing enough conflict can be hard imaginative work.

Once I sensed that I was simply tired, I refreshed my imagination by allowing it for a while to do just the opposite of what I usually asked it to do. Instead of dredging up new conflict possibilities, I decided *not* to put in conflict and obstacles.

What came out were the shortest "novels" in the world, like—

He always wanted her and he got her.

That's the end of that "novel."

or—

She had to escape and she did.

That's the end of that one.
or—

"Say yes!"
"Yes!"

Which ends that. Or one for the literati who love downers—

He was depressed so he killed himself.

I'm sure you get the point. Many would-be novelists make the narrative job much harder than it has to be by making life too easy for the hero. *Nothing in storytelling fails like letting the lead character succeed.* To put this another way: Good news for the viewpoint character is bad news for the author. And conversely: Bad news for the viewpoint character is good news for the author.

So, once the lead character has established a long-term goal, the reader forms an umbrella story question. Then you provide another character as the source of active conflict to make sure nothing comes easy for the lead, and the reader worries like hell and gets a tummy-ache and stays up half the night reading your novel—and loves it.

Look at your own novel. If you were to send it to me in its present form, would I know very early on:

- who the lead character is?
- what specifically he wants?
- why it's vital to his happiness?
- who stands between him and attainment?

I hope so.

But another word of warning: In real life we often confront opposition of a vast and amorphous kind. "Society" seems against us, or "church," or "popular opinion." In fiction, while the opposition may be powerful and broadspread, the dramaturgy works infinitely better if the lead character and the major source of opposition are *people*, not organizations or social entities or anything of that nature. A story is the playing out of a moral equation of some kind, and it's much more fun for the reader if she can identify the sides *in individual characters*.

I refer you again to the concept of putting your novel on a stage before a live audience. If your play opens with this huge, blobby brown *shape* coming out with a sign on its back, "Forces of unselfish good," and then entering stage left comes this long, slinky, creepy *other shape* labeled "bad guys in society," I don't think the audience is going to stay long.

People identify with people, not abstract concepts. Same in a novel, OK? Don't be vague. Don't be subtle. Give me people willing to struggle.

GOAL SELECTION

Well, all well and good, you may say. But how do I pick a goal for a lead character? How do I know it's important (big) enough? How do I know the reader won't yawn or think it's dumb?

Every writer has a chronic fear of writing something "dumb." The fear keeps a lot of writers well back from the edge, writing stuff that's safe or tried-and-true or the same thing you saw in a movie last year. This kind of fear, common as it is, is deadly. You have to be willing to risk being dumb. Chances are you won't be.

So how to pick a lead character's goal? To answer that question requires another brief excursion into psychology.

Fairly early in this century, when Freudians were doing their free association thing and Jung was developing his theory of the collective unconscious and Karen Horney was somewhere in the middleground, there was another psychologist at work in the northeastern United States whose name never became well known. But this man's basic theory is more useful to a novelist than most of the things done by the others just named.

The psychologist's name was Prescott Leckey, and essentially what he said was this: *Every human's most vital task in life is the preservation and enhancement of his concept of himself.* Or to put it another way, as was done years later by S.I. Hayakawa in his book, *Symbol, Status and Personality*: The primary goal of a human is not self-preservation, but preservation of the symbolic self.

Why else, Hayakawa asks, would a man spend $300 a year on equipment to catch $2 worth of fish? Or why would a young woman skip lunch for years to buy a fur coat, even today when some people think fur coats look better on their original woodland owners? Or—I might add—why would a soldier throw his body on a live grenade to save fellow soldiers he hardly knows, ensuring his own physical obliteration?

Leckey says we begin forming a self-concept very early in life. We test it, and if it seems reasonably accurate, we begin to define ourselves more specifically by it. "I'm a man of action." Or "I'm a woman of quality." Or "I'm a brilliant writer, but I can't do math." Once we start making such judgments about ourselves, the die is cast. We work to become more of what we are. Very often we do things, or refuse to do them, based on a judgment as to whether the action would be consistent with our self-concept.

The self-concept is that view of oneself, positive or negative, that is admissible to consciousness. Scratch a story character (or a real-life person) and she is apt to tell you something like, "I would never cheat on my income tax because I'm not that kind of person!" (whatever "kind of person" that is) or "I can't dance; I've always been clumsy and shy."

There is nothing mysterious or vague about the self-concept in terms of the unconscious or pre-conscious. The self-concept is known (if sometimes not carefully examined) by its holder, and people act on what they think they are—and aren't.

In real life, and in fiction, people generally don't like everything in their concept of themselves, but they've reached accommodations: The shy little girl writes poetry but stays out of school plays; The other little girl who defines herself as socially at ease and extroverted may shun poetry-writing, but will jump at any chance to perform. Joe grabs every chance to climb a cliff or ride a cycle or walk a ledge or swim in the quarry. Why does he take such risks? "I'm just that kind of guy," he'll tell you.

Self-concepts can be positive or negative. There's a story of a substitute teacher who went into a classroom of gifted children one week. She found they were outstanding in everything except math. They couldn't do *anything* in math.

Puzzled, the substitute teacher did some detective work and learned that an earlier teacher of this class had said one day in exasperation, "I've never seen a class like this one! You children just can't do math!"

The kids had taken the information in, and in a twinkling

it became part of their self-concept as a group. They were the class that couldn't do math. So of course they were unable to do math!

The substitute teacher took days, tricking the kids into doing word problems (which, having the self-concept of being good readers, they could of course do), and finally told them, "Hey, these word problems you've been doing are full of math. So you guys have changed. Now you are the class that can also do math!"

The class's self-concept changed, and the problem vanished.

So the self-concept, which often affects the person's present reality, is vitally important. We dress, work, play roles, buy cars, pick restaurants and friends, do some things and shun other activities—all because of who and what we think we are. We have a self-definition, and we do everything in our power to protect and enhance it.

All this according to Leckey.

THE SELF-CONCEPT AND CHARACTER MOTIVES

Do you see the relevance of self-concept to selection of story goal for a character? I hope so. Preservation of the symbolic self is our number one priority. If something will help the character repair a battered self-concept—or enhance an existing one—then that something will be essential to the character's happiness—and he will die to get it.

And so a man spends all his life searching for the identity of his real father, because he is the kind of man who believes he can never feel whole until he knows—because he is not the kind of man who gives up. Or a woman stays with a man who drinks, and beats her, because she is not the kind of woman who divorces. Or a villain begins a murderous round of visits to former jurors who sent him to prison because he is not the kind of man who forgives or forgets. None of these quests has to be logical by any standard outside that dictated by the self-concept of the given character.

The trick in planning problems in a novel—in matching problem with self-concept with goal—lies in finding either (1) a character for whom your planned problem will create a crisis, or (2) finding a problem that will threaten the self-concept of your planned character. Some writers start with character, some with plot. They all get to the same place.

Suppose, for example, we go back to the two young girls we mentioned earlier, the one who sees herself as a poet who shuns the spotlight, and the other who sees herself as socially easygoing and wonderful.

Now let's assume we want to write a story in which the teacher goes to a child in the class and says, "Millicent, I have wonderful news! You have been picked to sing at the school Christmas party, and do a little dance."

For little girl A, this plot premise is a disaster. After all, *she* is the little girl who can't do things like that. The idea of performing in public makes her sick. It doesn't fit her self-concept. She will immediately pick some plan—some goal—to get her out of the situation and restore her feeling of balance with her self-concept.

So for little girl A, this is a good plot, painful and filled with personal danger. She has a struggle ahead of her—she has to pick some goal to get through the crisis.

But what about little girl B? She thinks of herself as socially adept, remember. Given the same assignment, she sees no circumstance that threatens her self-concept in any way. "Great!" she says gleefully. "I'll bring my tutu. Can I play the harmonica too?" So for her, our plot idea doesn't work at all. She doesn't need to pick any new goal. She's happy just as she is.

That's what I mean when I say you start either with a plot, and find a character whose self-concept will be threatened by it, or you pick a character and then build up a plot that will be threatening. Mix and match. As long as you don't write about passive characters (and I've already mentioned that injunction in chapter five), then the character will form a goal, you will provide opposition and the story is under way.

During the writing of your novel, incidentally, characters may often further define themselves for the reader by stating—and even arguing about—their self-concept. We'll return to this idea in chapters twelve and thirteen.

So we have seen here how goal motivation, stemming from deeply felt needs for happiness, defines specifically and clearly what the lead character wants. The reader forms a story question from that, and has the suspense-curiosity umbrella that will sustain her interest through all the twists and turns in the longest plot—provided the climax is delayed again and again, through conflict.

WORKING ASSIGNMENT

Now here's an assignment for you.

Look at four or five published novels. Notice how goal comes up early, is repeated often, is confronted constantly by other people with opposing goals—conflict. Underline passages that stress these factors. Analyze how they are stated or introduced and developed—how they are repeated throughout the book. Make notes on different ways *you* can specify goal statement in your own book, keeping it in the reader's consciousness. Log your conclusions in your journal.

Because this is vital, let me suggest that you give yourself more "soak time" on the matter. You can read a book like this one straight through in a few hours, and thus be very efficient. The problem will be that you'll only register whatever you already know, and will miss everything that's new to you—*the very stuff you bought the book to learn.*

How can you avoid this? By taking the assignments seriously, and taking your time in doing them. By making notes in your journal. By meditating some more.

Slow down. If you don't want to do the work, just gestate for a few days and put in some time thinking about the color yellow. Or green. Or whatever.

Chapter Eight

How a Story Starts– and How It Ends

In his wonderful book, *The Ordeal of Change*, the late long-shoreman-philosopher Eric Hoffer tells about a time during the Great Depression of the 1930s when he was a migrant farm worker in the Pacific Northwest. Hoffer and his friends, it seems, were working for an hourly wage, picking a certain kind of vegetable.

One evening the foreman came to the workers and told them to get on the boxcars nearby because they were being taken to California, where they would pick a very similar—but different—vegetable.

Racketing down the west coast on the train that night, Hoffer noticed his companions in all kinds of discomfort. Perhaps they were drinking or fighting or looking morose—and Hoffer himself realized he was frightened and apprehensive.

This, he thought, was ridiculous. There simply wasn't much difference between picking, say, green beans and peas.

But then he had an insight that helped him understand. *We know we can pick green beans,* he thought. *But we don't know yet if we can pick peas.* And so he learned that virtually any change—however seemingly insignificant—can be threatening.

Remembering our earlier look at Prescott Leckey and the self-concept, we can understand why this should be true. We build an environment to support our self-concept. We act within the demands and limitations of that self-concept, and work to maintain the supportive environment we have created for ourselves. As long as things stay the same, we feel comfortable.

But enter change. *Any change.* The environment is subtly altered. We and our self-concept are no longer in harmony with it. We are uncomfortable—even scared.

That's why the best stories start with change. A stranger arrives in town. A new family moves in on the block. A marriage begins, or ends. A baby is born. The first leaves of autumn fall. A letter arrives. The telephone rings. Change hits the viewpoint character, and a story begins.

Notice in your reading of popular novels how often the moment of change is the moment the book begins. Notice, too, how often the seasoned professional—just to be sure the reader gets the message—will actually use the word "change" in the first page or two of the novel.

Change means lack of harmony with the environment—a threat to the self-concept. Since the self-concept is our most precious possession, we will fight to protect it, to find a new harmony. We will do *something*. The same is true for a story character confronted by change. If she is worth writing about— an active rather than passive character—she will try to make things right again, to cope with the change.

She will, in other words, pick a goal vital to her happiness.

This goal becomes the story goal, and the reader will see the story question in that—and begin to worry about it. And we are off on a promising story, having started at the right time and place.

As you think about your novel and your main viewpoint character, review what you know about change and the self-concept, and think deeply about how to open your story with this crucial time of threatening change.

NEVER WARM UP YOUR ENGINES

Remember that the story should *start* with this change. It is not necessary to provide the reader with a boring depiction of the status quo before you change it. Get the change shown as swiftly as possible and show the character beginning to react with predictable unease—or worse. You can always explain details of the pre-story situation later.

This is quite important. I've often had the experience of sitting down with a student manuscript and being confronted by a long recitation of story backdrop, or lengthy description of the setting, or analysis of a character before the character gets onstage. When I wake up later and ask the student why he started in such a dull manner, he always says with a frown,

"Well, there was all this stuff I had to set up."

All such "stuff" amounts to warming up your creative engines. It has no place starting your actual manuscript. Drivers warm up their engines before the start of a motor race, too. But nobody comes to see that.

Most of the things you think you need to "set up" are author concerns. The reader doesn't care. He wants the story to start.

So *start* it. Get the reader hooked and worry about backstory later.

THE THREAT SHOULD BE CLEAR

Of course there can be plot situations in which you might want to show the threatening change being set up before your main character becomes fully aware of it. That's fine too. You might, for example, open your book with a brief prologue or very brief first chapter in which the villain of the piece is introduced and shown setting up the dastardly deed that will change things for the main character. Or you might show something mysterious happening, then switch to the main character; in such a case, your reader will feel sure that the mysterious happening relates to the hero and represents a threatening change about to befall him.

With either of these approaches that start outside the awareness of the major viewpoint, the justification must be that this approach more clearly and swiftly makes the reader aware that a threatening change is taking place. So occasionally—to make absolutely certain that the change is demonstrated as early as possible—you will read a novel that starts somewhere other than the main character's viewpoint.

It's important to remember in such cases that the nonstandard opening was not selected to be cute or to warm up the motors, but to get the change onto the page as early as possible, even at risk of waiting a few pages to establish the primary viewpoint of the novel.

Another method involves a simple topic sentence or paragraph. Most of us can remember some novel we've read in the past which began with a sentence like, "It began as a normal day, and he had no idea that by nightfall his world would be upside down." The writer, having started with a sentence like this, can get away with a bit of "normal day" activity on a few following pages because the reader is already hooked by the promise of the change.

Or consider this opening from John D. MacDonald's novel, *Darker Than Amber*, often mentioned by novelists when they get together and chat about favorites:

> We were about to give up and call it a night when somebody dropped the girl off the bridge.

Professionals love to open a book and read a starting sentence like that. They know they are in the hands of a fellow pro who will be entertaining. Everyday readers love such an opening, too, although they may not know the theory behind it.

Your novel may not have such a dramatic start. But you can identify the threat or hook that is inherent in your opening situation, and you can hit the reader with it *at once*.

Remember, your first reader will be the jaded editor. You have perhaps twenty-five words to engage her interest.

KEEPING CHARACTER CONFUSION TO A MINIMUM

Sometimes, in opening a novel, we want to get a lot of things moving fast. We want to establish that threat, start several subplots and get several colorful characters onstage as fast as we can.

Those are all good impulses. But we can have too much of a good thing. If you dump too much on the reader all at once, confusion can result.

This is especially true with introducing characters. That's because the reader starts the book knowing *no one* in it. It takes a while, usually, for the author to establish who Frank is, and how he's different from Bill, and what role each is playing in the story. Add Jim and Bart and Dan and Sally and Nancy and Kim and Brett—and try to throw them all into the opening chapter along with the primary change—and "confusion" may not be a strong enough word to describe what happens in the reader's mind.

How to avoid this potential problem? You simply set up your plot so that you can introduce your characters *one or two at a time*.

For example, if you plan a first scene in which the threatening change comes out in a dinner conversation, and your imagination sees Jack and Linda and Sally and Bill and Arnold at the table, the reader may well be swamped with too much character "input" and be confused. This is especially true at the start of a novel, where you are also trying to establish time and locale.

The solution to such a potential problem is self-evident. Several of your imagined dinner guests have to be late, or leave early, or go into the adjacent room so that Jack and Linda are alone while he tells her that the bank has just foreclosed on the loan, or whatever.

To put this another way: Often you have to plot to get clutter-characters offstage for the sake of clarity. Mob scenes are always hard to write and potentially confusing, particularly at the outset of a novel. Whenever possible, *set up a one-to-one situation.*

To summarize about starting your novel:

1. Start with a threat to the lead character's self-concept.
2. Make it clear and simple.
3. Worry about backstory later.
4. Look for the most vivid words that will hook the reader.
5. Set up one-to-one scenes to avoid confusion.

Remember that your goal on the first page is to *get the editor to read the second*! Everything else can come later.

HOW TO END THE NOVEL

Of course the ending of your novel must, first and foremost, answer the story question. Remember that you started the book with a change that threatened the character's self-concept, and as a result she formed a long-term goal—something she would achieve or discover or decide on that would fix things; the reader has turned this goal statement into a story question, and has worried about it for hundreds of pages. You must answer it!

You may do this by something as simple as letting Linda finally find a new loan to replace the one that was foreclosed in chapter one. Or you might have your hero toss villain Jeb off the roof. However you do it, it often helps to think of a story plot as a moral equation, a concept mentioned in chapter three.

In that chapter I mentioned that William Foster-Harris, once a great writing teacher at the University of Oklahoma, held to this idea. He said the forces at war in most stories were moral or ethical issues, and often could be expressed as something like:

love + greed =

So Foster-Harris believed that the end of the novel not only had to answer the story question, but ought to show a clear decision between warring principles.

For in-depth discussion of this point, you should consult Foster-Harris's book on the subject. Here, it's enough to restate that Foster-Harris saw every story as the record of a war dealing with internal—as well as external—forces, a battle between opposing ideals or loyalties.

Foster-Harris's favorite example was a story of an old man in ancient times who, far past the age for fathering children, had a son whom he loved beyond all else on earth. But the old man, who had spent his long life loving and honoring his God, was called by the voice of God one day to take his son to the top of a mountain. Once there, the old man heard God tell him to sacrifice the son to prove his love for Him.

In this case (roughly the story of Abraham and Isaac in the Bible), the old man was confronted with the cruelest dilemma: he had to make a choice between love of his God and love of his son.

In Foster-Harris's terms:

(Parental Love) versus (Love for God) will end with–

Or—

(PL) + (LG) = ?

It was Foster-Harris's contention that most of the great stories of all time somehow take part in this archetypal pattern of having plot finally devolve to a moment where the central character is forced to the ultimate moral dilemma, where no choice looks good and circumstance absolutely forces the character to make a decision *in action, now, and based on who and what he ultimately is.*

Such a test in the climax of a story (of whatever length) is the final crisis and test of the worth of the character. Surely, if the story has been of a sympathetic character, we as readers want the character to make the "good" choice. But—as in the case of the Hebrew readers of the story of Abraham—the "good" decision may appear to be *sacrificial*—in Abraham's case, literally so.

There is no doubt that to early readers (or hearers) of the Abraham story, the "good" decision was to sacrifice Isaac. But this was also clearly a sacrifice in more ways than one. Abraham evidently stood to lose everything by so doing: his beloved son, his future as a progenitor of the race, his daily happiness. And what could he see that he might get? Nothing!

This moral equation became Abraham's ultimate test, the final proof (in the story) as to whether he was admirable, lovable, worthy of our reader concern. In such stories, we writhe in agony with the character facing such a dilemma.

Abraham, as told in the Bible story, tried to delay a decision about his dilemma. God would have none of it, and demanded a decision at once. At this moment, Abraham became the sum total of who and what he was. He made no speeches, consulted no standard references, gave no sermons, *but simply showed his decision in action.*

He raised his hand to slay his beloved son, Isaac. At which point his Hebrew onlookers must have been filled with love and admiration—and horror. After all, here he was, doing the right thing, and he was surely about to lose everything.

Such a moment of horror and fear in the reader is the ultimate goal of the writer at the climax. We know now that the character is admirable and deserving. He has proven it. But in this dark moment after the decision, it appears he will lose all precisely because he has made the right choice—giving us the morally and spiritually uplifting and affirmative answer to his story equation:

(Parental Love) + (Love of God) = Love of God

But now, says Foster-Harris, if Abraham slays his son and loses all, then what has the story proved about the human condition? That good choices mean nothing; that life is random and cruel; that selfishness is better than principle. And none of that is good because most fiction, based on a moral equation, is at some level an affirmation of traditional values and a statement that life is worth living truly and honestly—and that good is rewarded. Art, like religion, is life-affirming.

Therefore—as in the story of Abraham—there must be a reversal. In the Bible story, God stays Abraham's hand. He says it was a test of Abraham's love for Him. So we breathe a sigh of relief at this reversal of our expectations, this unforeseen turn of events. Isaac is spared. And then we think, "But of course! I didn't see it before, but Abraham's God would never have really asked him to sacrifice Isaac! I should have seen that it was a test!"

So the sacrificial decision is followed by a dark moment, which is followed by a reversal—which is both *logical and unanticipated*. And this in itself is tremendously satisfying.

But note, please, that the ancient teller of the Abraham tale did not stop there. Abraham not only gets what he thought he was about to lose—his son—but God tells him, in effect, "Since you have proven your great love for me, I will name you to lead My people, and your seed will endure forever."

Kingship, in effect—and immortality. Rewards far beyond Abraham's wildest dreams—and far more than he thought he would have when he earlier chose the "bad" decision about sacrificing Isaac—and all because he made the right instinctive choice. So life and decency are affirmed, and the human condition validated.

All novels may not work with plot and character materials that lend themselves to a climax involving sacrifice and reversal. But if you will analyze any dozen popular novels, you are sure to find elements of sacrifice by the major character *throughout* each novel. And in at least half of those books, the climax will indeed involve the viewpoint character with his back to the wall, forced to an ultimate, cruel moral dilemma (which illustrates the equation), a decision shown in action (which makes the decision concrete and dramatic), a dark moment (which tatters the reader's confidence and makes him shake) and a reversal that is simply wonderfully satisfying (bringing out the affirmative theme).

In bad fiction, the plot and people are manipulated to bring about the desired end. In good fiction, it seems inevitable. What's the difference? Author skill and hard work.

Look at your plot materials and how you plan to end your story. Find an ultimate test. Set up the background and the character goals, needs and assumptions so that, hidden inside the seeming disaster lie the fruits of glory. Play the scene for all it's worth—which is everything, since this is your ultimate proof that the character is worth saving. And then—bring out your theme without preaching by showing the dynamic reversal of expectations, both the character's and your reader's.

The process is fundamental to how we learn all the most significant things in our life. Fantasy, some think, is the process by which we remember our yesterdays, and story is the process by which we create a unity out of the chaos of existence.

THE RIGHT ENDING–NOT A FAKE HAPPY ONE

Does the idea of a happy ending worry you? It needn't. People read for affirmation, inspiration, escape, assurance that life is basically worth living—at least some of the time—and they do not read to learn more about the humdrum, the routine, the dull or the discouraging. None of those things are what art is about. So you needn't worry, and your ending needn't be phony if you exercise your judgment, compassion and skill.

Or you may assuage your worry about happy endings by turning the equation upside down—by showing a less-than-admirable character *making the selfish choice* in order to win everything. And then, of course, that character loses because, hidden in the situation were the seeds of destruction he could not see through his selfishness.

Let me repeat: All stories are not told this way. But most of the best ones are.

Consider the ramifications of the philosophical point of view and their technical implications. Don't, please, think you're too cynical, smart, worldly-wise or sophisticated to use as best you can this view of how a story ends.

In chapter sixteen, especially, we'll return to the matter of novel endings when we take a long look at general novel structure. In the meantime, it may be comforting for you to realize that *starting right* puts you halfway there on the journey to *ending right*. And now, if for heaven's sake you'll be sure not to start thinking you have to be subtle about story goal or the story question, you're on your way.

It wouldn't hurt at this point to look over a half-dozen recent novels in terms of how they open. With a colored pencil, find and mark the words or paragraphs that spell out the threatening change. If you are willing to take the time, skip through one or two of these books and mark all the places where the change, the resulting goal and complications flowing out of that struggle are made clear again. Turn to the ending. Mark the words that answer the story question. See if you can find a moral dilemma involved.

Then take perhaps the hardest—but most vital—step. Open your work journal. Write down at least six positive conclusions you've drawn from the exercise to anchor your understanding and ensure that you won't soon forget it.

These may take any form you wish, of course. You might copy a particularly neat opening. Or you might jot down two or three succinct topic sentence "hooks" that have occurred to you. Or you might write down why you think Writer A opens more strongly than Writer B.

Students sometimes complain that they just can't think of a positive conclusion. They aren't thinking hard enough. We're not asking for nuclear physics here. We just want words in the journal that represent the best ideas and conclusions you can come up with. Do it! It's important.

Chapter Nine

Scene and Sequel

Y ou are embarking on a long chapter. It is, in my opinion, the single most important in this book,
If you have been carefully studying earlier chapters
and fully understand them, then this one will provide
you with the theory that can make everything start to come
together for you as a novelist. So, even though this chapter is
a long one, *don't* fall prey to the temptation to hurry through
it.

Perhaps I feel so strongly about this because it was only
when I learned about scene and sequel that I was able to start
my own selling career. For me, it made all the difference. So
I tend to think it can make all the difference for you, too.

The late Dwight V. Swain was the teacher who made it
clear for me. His book, *Techniques of the Selling Writer*, remains
one of the best ever written on all aspects of storywriting. Get
it. Read it.

It was Swain, many years ago, who pounded scene structure
into me in individual conferences over a period of three years.
He kept telling me the same thing, and I kept assuring him I
understood perfectly—then I kept going off and writing more
chapters which proved again and again that I only imagined I
understood. Swain, bless him, kept on pounding.

Finally I saw the light. I still remember the flash of insight.
"So *that's* what he's been saying!" I cried. And went off and
wrote a novel that sold. And fourteen more in succession.

Learning about scene and sequel structure has been a lifelong pursuit for me. There is so much involved in it, if you
get deeply into the subject, that I wrote an entire book on
scene and structure alone (*Scene and Structure*, published by

Writer's Digest Books). There is nothing I more enjoy talking about at workshops, because I know if writers get the basic points, they're on their way.

Let's look at the basic points.

THE NATURE OF SCENE

People read novels to escape the reality of their everyday, humdrum, sometimes-depressing lives. They look for entertainment, thought-provoking ideals, colorful locales and involvement with the story people through their imagination.

To put it in a word, readers read for *excitement* of some kind.

To provide the reader her excitement, you have to have a story to tell. You have to have good characters. You have to have feeling. But above all else you have to have a *storytelling structure* that provides a lifelike reading experience.

Four characteristics of our experience of real life are:

1. It is lived moment-by-moment, with *no* summary.
2. It is lived from a single viewpoint.
3. It is lived *now*.
4. It is lived with the knowledge that what we do has results.

Therefore, it seems only logical that we would want to put as much of our novel as possible in the same kind of framework.

That's why we have scene—a component of the story which plays out in the story now, from a single viewpoint, told moment-by-moment, with no summary—and what the characters do has what I have earlier called "downstream effects," impact on later developments which determine the course of the rest of the story.

A problem, however, immediately becomes apparent. If we try to tell all of our novel moment-by-moment, even the shortest tale will become hopelessly long. The writing-down of any hour of your life—even a dull hour—with no summary of any kind might fill a volume. And in real life we sort of summarize by daydreaming, nodding off, paying little attention for a while.

So everything in a novel cannot be a scene.

That's one of the reasons we have the other component of story, the sequel. We'll look at the sequel later in this chapter. For now, however, let's start with the structure of the scene.

SCENE STRUCTURE

Scene provides excitement and involvement. Its structure is threefold:

GOAL
CONFLICT
DISASTER

Just as a story starts with statement of a character's long-term goal, so every scene starts with a character—usually the viewpoint character—saying very specifically what he wants to accomplish in the confrontation about to take place. This subsidiary goal relates—is a stepping-stone somehow—to the long-term story goal. And just as the reader will translate a story goal into a story question, and worry about it, he will just as readily formulate a *scene question*, and worry about that, seeing as he will that the scene goal relates to the long-term story question.

The scene goal can be stated by having the character say it out loud beforehand—

> "Mickey, I'm going in there and I have *got* to convince Bigley to let me off early so I can go to night school two nights a week."

Or it can be stated in character thought—

> Walking into Bigley's office, Cliff knew he had to convince Bigley to let him off early two nights a week.

Or it can be stated or paraphrased in the opening lines of the scene after earlier notice to the reader—

> "Mister Bigley, I'm here to convince you that it's vital for me to get off work early two nights a week. I think it will be a good thing for the company, too."

Sometimes (although this tactic can be risky) the goal of your new scene can be set up clearly in whatever action immediately precedes it. So, for example, suppose you show two people in a car wreck; one of the passengers, Donna, says to Robin, "I'm hurt! You have to get help!" Now if you show Robin arguing with the nearby grumpy farmer, begging him to allow use of his telephone, the reader already has a good idea that Robin's goal is to call for help. Even in such an obvious situation, however, experienced novelists often repeat the goal—to get help—because reader understanding of the goal is all-important.

CLARITY OF GOAL IS EVERYTHING

Good novelists never write a scene where the goal is vague or ambiguous. They never make the mistake of trying to be subtle about it. The reader has to know what's wanted in no uncertain terms. So good writers leave no doubt about it. They write so that the goal in every scene is perfectly clear, specific and possibly obtainable right now.

This seems obvious once you get the hang of it. But far too many beginning novelists yearn to be subtle. "Wouldn't it be neater to let the reader sort of figure out the goal as she reads along?" they ask.

No!

Imagine that you go to a football game, you climb into the stands and are confronted by an endless gridiron, extending over the horizon to the south on your right, the north on your left. At the time of the kickoff, you see the start of the game. But suppose the visiting team immediately starts a drive—and drives right out of sight to the north.

You sit and wait, totally uninvolved and confused.

Maybe a little later you see one of the home team's halfbacks churn over the far horizon, chug past the stands, and then disappear over the horizon to the south. "What *is* this?" you would cry. "I don't know what's going on! This is crazy! I'm getting out of here!"

Why? No goals in sight. So the game could not possibly make sense.

That's the way it works in a scene, too. The goal must be stated specifically and clearly. And it must come at the start.

CONFLICT: THE MAJOR ELEMENT

We say that the format of the scene is goal, conflict and disaster, but this is not to imply they represent equal portions of a scene. Actually, the goal may be stated in a few words, then reiterated several times in only a few more. A great percentage of the scene is the conflict portion.

Once the viewpoint character's goal has been stated, someone has to come along at once and say, in effect, "Huh-uh. You're not getting that, and I'm here to stop you." This antagonist, too, is strongly motivated because he sees how this scene fits into his struggle against the hero—how the outcome of this confrontation fits into *his* game plan. And so a struggle starts.

(Once in a while the antagonist to the viewpoint character can start a scene by coming in and stating *his* goal—which the viewpoint character must then try to thwart. But you will remember from earlier chapters that it's far better, almost all the time, to have the viewpoint character driving the action, trying to attain, rather than being passive or merely reactive. So, usually, in this scene-step the viewpoint character has to have a plan and be trying to attain toward its fulfillment.)

So you have a clear, stated goal and an opposing figure. Conflict is started. And since readers love conflict for its excitement, you want to develop it. How? Moment by moment, with no summary. Like real life. How do you manage to tell things moment by moment? By showing stimulus-and-response transactions.

The two fighters feint and parry, maneuver, try variations of their game plan, try to gain advantage, *reveal their character in what they say and do under pressure*, and fight to win. There is no summary—intended or inadvertent—because we want this to be as lifelike as possible, and there's no summary in real life.

Not long ago, it was common for major scenes in novels to extend ten or twenty pages. Today it is more common for them to be briefer and more intense. But there still is no summary, and the major angles in the conflict of the moment must be explored.

Sooner or later, however, the fight has been staged, all the maneuvers have been tried and the scene is to end. How does it end? With disaster.

THE NATURE OF DISASTER

If Cliff goes into Bigley's office intent on getting permission to leave early two nights a week, should we end the scene with his getting what he came after?

Absolutely not! In storytelling terms, good news is always bad tactics—bad news always good. After all, if events in this novel have downstream effects—and everything is tied tightly together—and the goal in this scene relates to Cliff's story quest, then if he gets this goal, he's happy, everything is going fine, he's on his way to getting what he wants in the long run— and there is no reader suspense or tension. Which means the story just failed. So the scene cannot end well for poor Cliff. There must be a setback, a disaster. And it must be of a very special kind. It must be a logical but unanticipated turn of events by which Cliff, by struggling to attain something good and worthwhile *and as a result of having tried so hard*, gets anything but what he wants. So as a result of having struggled manfully he is farther behind the eight ball than ever.

"This is awful!" the reader thinks. "I feel bad for Cliff! I feel sorry for him! Damn, I want him to win, but I don't think he can, now! I feel terrible and worried and filled with suspense.

"What a great novel this is! I can't put it down!"

But to work well, the disaster cannot be just any bad news the lazy writer wants to shovel in. It has to fit.

Suppose Cliff goes in and tells Bigley he wants time off. Bigley says no. They argue and maneuver. At the end, you need a disaster. So you have somebody rush in and say the plant is on fire. No, no, no. No good at all. Why? Because this disaster is like dropping an alligator over the transom. It has nothing to do with the fight that just took place.

To work, the disaster must be organic. That is, it must grow logically out of what has been going on in the scene. Or to put this another way: Every scene starts with goal, and the goal statement raises a scene question in the reader's mind. This question must always be one that can be answered simply in terms of the goal. The only possible answers are:

YES
NO
YES, BUT!
NO, AND FURTHERMORE!

But we've already seen that, while possible, the "Yes" answer destroys all reader tension and probably kills off your story because the hero is suddenly happy and on his way to see the Wizard. So the scene question has to be answered "No," "Yes, but!" or "No, and furthermore!" And this answer has to be logical but unanticipated, and it has to make the viewpoint character's situation a lot worse.

For example, let's look at poor Cliff again.

Suppose that a central value of Cliff's life is that he must be a good provider for his young sister, whom he supports. His concept of himself is of a responsible, hardworking older brother. His entire life has been centered around the idea of being a good provider and fulfilling family responsibilities.

Cliff has decided that, in order to be a good brother, he has to have a good office job with Bigley Wrench Company. But to get a good office job, he has to become an accountant. In order to become an accountant, he has to go to night school. In order to go to night school, he has to have two evenings off early each week. In order to get the time off, he has to convince Bigley.

So he goes into this meeting dedicated to his goal. It is essential to his self-concept, and so to his happiness.

He tells Bigley what he wants. Bigley demurs. Cliff argues fervently. Bigley grows irritated. Seeing his dream slipping away, Cliff presses the fight, becoming eloquent. The two men struggle, argue, maneuver.

Finally comes the climax of the scene. We want a disaster. We can have Bigley say:

"Cliff, I've heard enough! For the last time, my answer is NO! Now get out of this office!"

This is a good "no" disaster. But it's not great. Cliff leaves the scene in essentially no worse shape than he was going in. Not much has changed. His problem has grown no worse. He is no more desperate, in no additional trouble. There really hasn't been much dramatic "progress."

So a "no" answer is good, but often you need even more than that.

Let's play the scene again. Same stuff. At the end, let's have Bigley become cunning and say:

"Okay, Cliff. I'm not convinced. But let's put it this

way. I'm a reasonable man. My answer is *yes, but* you have to work twelve hours both Saturdays and Sundays to make up for it. Which means you'll never get to spend any time with your sister, or studying."

This is better. Did Cliff get what he wanted? *Yes, but*! He staggers out of the office in worse shape—with more problems—than when he went in to fight the good fight.

A lot of scenes end this way in working fiction. Usually they have the added beneficial result of forcing the viewpoint character into some new scene or series of scenes (new plot) as he tries to cope with the dimensions of the new and unexpected disaster.

But perhaps there is an even stronger way.

Same scene. Bigley gets more and more impatient, finally angry. At the end he shouts:

"Damn it, Cliff! For the tenth time, the answer is *No*! *And furthermore*, you have made me so angry with your arguing that I've had it with you. You've pushed me too far. You're fired!"

This is grand. Now we've done something really good. Cliff staggers out a wreck, having lost everything because he tried to work toward a worthwhile goal. *He brought on his own disaster.* He tried to reach a laudable goal, but not only failed to reach the short-term goal, but made his situation worse. Now he has no job—which more keenly threatens his self-concept as a good breadwinner.

This is story "progress." The best and most dramatic scenes work like this. We make our story go forward by pushing our hero backward, farther and farther from his ultimate goal, through scene disaster. The reader reads excitedly, roots for the hero—and then is crushed with him.

And the novel flies along, lifelike, dramatic, filled with suspense, hard to put down, filled with twists and surprises and setbacks—and more and more tension as well as admiration for the battered hero, who simply won't quit.

THE STRUCTURE OF SEQUEL

Now that we've built the suspense, what happens with Cliff as he leaves Bigley's factory for the last time?

"My God!" he cries, clapping his hand to his forehead. "I feel shocked and scared and angry and terrible! What can I possibly do now? No avenue looks good! I've got to think about this. Let me see . . . where did I go wrong . . . what can I do now? I guess I'll go down the street and try to get a job at Acme Tool." And he starts down the street.

That, in a nutshell, is the pattern of sequel:

EMOTION
QUANDARY
DECISION
ACTION

It's the way we react to any disaster in real life. First: blind emotional reaction. Later, a struggle to think again, but confusion, where possibly no course of action looks very good. Finally, a new decision, maybe not very good, but the best we can come up with. And then new action based on that decision.

The nature of scene is excitement. But the nature of sequel is logic, with emotion and characterization thrown in. Sequel allows summary, transition, skipped time. It is where the character reacts to what just took place (the disaster), looks at his options, plans something to try next and gets going again.

Some sequels may be as short as the one we imagined poor old Cliff going through. Some may go on a long time indeed. Scene is swift-moving and involving, but there isn't a lot of room for thought, except as part of quick stimulus-response internalizations. Sequel is slow-moving and possibly emotional, and there is time for thought and feeling.

In a slam-bang action adventure novel, the entire sequel, after the mad killer hits the hero in the head with a meat-ax, might be something like this:

Bart's skull hurt like hell. "Damn, that makes me mad!" Bart thought. "I'm going to kill that sucker!" And he hurled himself back into the fight.

A book filled with such brief sequels reads breathlessly, at a wild pace, with never a major letup in the scene action.

In a novel like Saul Bellow's *Herzog*, on the other hand, Amos Herzog spends most of a long book in sequel to a scene or scenes *that played before the novel ever opened*. The result for a novelist of Bellow's talent is a long, thoughtful, evocative novel.

So how you play sequel depends on the situation, your intent as a writer, your authorial bent and architectonic demands of the moment, in view of the pace of your entire novel's structure.

We can, however, make some points about each segment of the sequel, even if you must decide how long any section should be—and, indeed, whether some sections are to play out on the page at all.

THE SEGMENTS OF THE SEQUEL

The first part of the natural reaction cycle is *emotion*. Pure feeling, with little thought possible just yet. This period may be as brief as it is in the exaggerated example about Bart just above. Or it may extend for many story hours, days or weeks—many manuscript pages or chapters.

The length of time devoted to the emotional reaction will depend on the kind of character you're writing about and the kind of plot. A tough, self-disciplined Marine Corps officer might allow himself very little emotion, and if he were in an action story where you had to get on with the plot, the emotion portion of the sequel might be very brief indeed. On the other hand, a highly emotional woman in a love story, where the reader interest is centered precisely on emotion, might be given many pages of sensitive rendition of her feelings.

The emotional segment of the sequel, like its other parts, may be rendered by the author's getting into the character's heart and describing the feelings directly. The description of emotion might be more cool, almost clinical, as the author "backs away" a bit from trying to describe the feelings directly. It might be portrayed by having the sequel character talk with another story person and tell how she is feeling. You'll find examples of each approach in your writing, and others in addition. I hope you'll look for them, mark them and make notes of your findings and impressions in your work journal.

Writing the emotion segment of sequel is the most dangerous place for a writer who tends to get carried away and write purple, hysterical prose. Therefore, many contemporary writers tend to cool their approach to emotion in sequel, and press on as quickly as possible.

Also, a person overwhelmed by emotion is always either paralyzed or acting crazy. Neither state moves the story forward very much. For this reason, too, the emotional compartment of the sequel has to end at some point, and the character has to start thinking again.

This *quandary* section usually takes a three-part form. The character "raps" with himself, going through Review, then Analysis, and finally Planning.

The character thinks, in effect, "I've got to review what this disaster means ... analyze what went wrong. ... try to formulate a new plan to get my quest back on track somehow." Not all three parts are always played and, as in other parts of the sequel, the process may be short or long, depending on circumstance.

This much can be said, however. After a disaster, prototypically the character reviews not only how the last disaster took place and what it means; she also recalls and reviews at least some of her earlier setbacks, trying to put everything together. These often-painful reviews by the viewpoint character put things in perspective for the reader, too, and are wonderful focusing devices that keep the long-term story question in clear view and point out what's significant.

After reviewing, the character starts analyzing her situation, and often is struck by at least a sense of dilemma—of seeing two possible courses of new action, neither of which looks very good. More often, the "dilemma" quickly becomes a quandary as—with the character—you the author show the thought process by which the character continues to analyze her plight.

This is the place where your character really plots the next stage of your novel for you. She considers doing this or that, but finds problems with any conceivable new plan. But, being so dedicated to her long-term quest, she moves on toward making a new action decision, ideal or not. Her thought processes, courage (or lack of it), ingenuity, demonstrated devotion to the cause and intelligence all characterize her as she struggles.

Finally—after perhaps only a page, perhaps after many more—she makes her new *decision*. She selects what she will do and commits to this new plan and goal.

She moves into her newly chosen plan. She takes *action*. She goes somewhere and does something, and reiterates her newly chosen goal. Then someone confronts her in conflict. And where are you? In the next scene.

Scene leads to sequel leads to scene leads to sequel. *This is the structure of long fiction that tells a story.* And of course from my biased standpoint there is no other kind.

DISTINGUISHING SCENE OR SEQUEL FROM INCIDENT

People will argue that everything that happens in a novel cannot be cast into the structure of a scene, and that every feeling-thoughtful passage is not necessarily a sequel. This is true; there are incidents without real meaning—with no downstream effects—in a novel. There may be hundreds of them. But accomplished novelists are always alert to see if they can make more of some incidents—if they can perhaps turn some into small scenes, at least, with subtle disasters or twists at the end. You can, too, if you try.

The key to turning dead-end incidents into dramatic scenes often lies in searching back to the opening of your existing incident and *searching for an implied intention* in the viewpoint character. If you can detect one, you may find it possible to emphasize and clarify that subtle intention, making it into a goal worthy of scenic development.

For example: I had a friend who wrote a long incident about a schoolteacher with high school kids on a tour abroad. The way my friend originally wrote it, the female viewpoint character ordered the bus driver to take them to a big castle on the hill, as planned in the tourbook. When the bus arrived, the woman got off, went to the door and met a cranky, sinister older man who said they could stay the night as planned, but wouldn't enjoy it.

This sequence of events seemed flat and undramatic, a mere incident. It just sort of sat there on the page.

I suggested to my friend that she make the incident into a scene.

"I don't write scenes!" she wailed. "I can't!"

After we fixed *that* self-concept problem, her revision was cast like this:

Same basic situation, same heroine. But now, the heroine

noticed as the bus approached the castle that some of the kids were nervous and cranky, perhaps scared of the old castle. So the heroine *formed the intention* of persuading them that staying the night would be fun. With this goal in mind, she walked up to the door of the castle. When the sinister man appeared, she stated her goal of making the visit fun; she urged the man to help her reassure the kids by coming down to the bus and talking to them. The man argued; she insisted. Finally he marched down to the bus and said, in effect, "There's nothing to worry about. The police believe that the man who killed seven students here last week is no longer in the immediate area."

So in the revision the goal was: *Get the man to talk to the kids to reassure them.*

The question thus became: *Will the heroine get the man to talk to the kids to reassure them?*

But the disaster thus became: *Yes, but as a result of her efforts, the man went down and scared all of them a lot more—including her.*

So the heroine marched into the castle feeling much worse than she would have if she hadn't tried to do anything at all, and as a result of *that*, (in sequel) she decided to take the kids on a fun sidetrip the next day, *but.* . . .

I hope you begin to get the picture.

Developing good, disastrous scenes will tax your ingenuity. But success can make your novel fascinating.

Writing good sequels will put you and the reader in closer touch with the viewpoint character and lay out future developments in the novel, while also, perhaps, patching up story logic and motivation.

CONTROLLING STORY PACE

Scenes, remember, are fast and involving. They make the story fly. Sequels are slower by nature—they slow the pace of your story down.

Therefore, it stands to reason that *you can control the pace of your story by manipulation of scene and sequel.* If the story is proceeding at too breakneck a speed, you lengthen a sequel here and there. If it's going too slowly, you expand scenes and shorten or even leave out some sequels.

REVIEW OF KEY POINTS

Because it is so important, please bear with me during a brief capsule review of this chapter's primary points.

- The scene is the dramatic segment of your novel in which you provide the reader with excitement.
- Excitement is provided through conflict over goal-motivated actions.
- The goal must be clear and immediate.
- The answer to the scene question raised by the goal statement should be one that can be answered "Yes," "No," "Yes, but!" or "No, and furthermore!"
- The scene is told moment-by-moment, without summary, using the technique of stimulus and response.
- The disaster ending the scene must answer the scene question.
- The disaster must be organic.
- The sequel is that component in which logic, emotion and story planning take place in reaction to the disaster.
- Sequel allows summary or the skipping of time.
- All or only some of a sequel's usual components can be presented, depending on writer need, story situation and pacing demands.
- Story pace can be controlled by manipulation of scene and sequel.

If you feel at all unsure about any of these points, or others that were raised in the chapter, you should review before going further.

IMPORTANT WORK TO BE DONE

In addition, you should practice planning sequences of scenes and sequels. You could use 3×5 or 5×7 cards, for example, in the following way:

Label the first card Scene No. 1. Write the name of the viewpoint character, his scene goal, his antagonist and at least three steps in the conflict. Then write in ten words or less what organic disaster ends this scene.

Label the second card Sequel No. 1. Write the same viewpoint character's name. Then pinpoint in a very few words how he feels emotionally as a result of the disaster that just took place;

what he thinks about as he reviews and starts trying to plan; and what new decision he takes, which leads to new action.

Label the third card Scene No. 2. Write the name of the same viewpoint character and state his new-scene goal which he just decided upon at the end of Sequel No. 1. Identify the new antagonist. Repeat the remaining steps noted for Scene No. 1.

Label the fourth card Sequel No. 2. Outline the sequel in the same way you outlined Sequel No. 1.

You should not consider this practice assignment completed until you have planned at least ten scenes with their following sequels, *and these should follow one another in a straight-line development of plot.*

It doesn't matter if you take material from your current novel project and plan it this way, or start afresh with a new character and idea and work out your learning project with those. The point is that you can't get by on abstract understanding of scene and sequel. You have to wrestle with the concepts, bang your head against the wall a few times, force yourself to keep trying—and so finally begin to feel how the process truly works.

In addition, following up on your newly found lifetime habit of analyzing written work in order to learn from it, you should dig out your colored pencils again.

Pick up one or two novels you read recently and liked. Go through them carefully, marking up big segments of them (if not all of them) to see how the writer handled scene and sequel.

> Look for scenes.
> Mark each goal statement in RED.
> Bracket each conflict section in BLUE.
> Highlight identifiable twists and steps in that conflict in YELLOW.
> Mark each disaster in BLACK.
> Look for sequels. Use other colors to mark each component part of each sequel that you can find. If some parts of a sequel are not to be found, you might ask yourself if you can figure out why.

Having done all this work, you should have material aplenty to log in your work journal!

A WORD OF WARNING . . . AND PROMISE

Finally, we can't leave this first excursion into scene and sequel structure without noting that you may, as you analyze published novels, find scenes in which—despite everything Mr. Bickham has said—the viewpoint does shift from one character to another and perhaps back again. This sometimes represents a very advanced technique, used for very special purposes. It's one of the things that will be considered in chapter sixteen.

But you don't want to start trying such an advanced technique just yet, unless you've already published a few novels. Many fine, popular books are published every year with a single viewpoint represented throughout. Practice limiting your viewpoint at least within every given scene. This discipline will give you scenes that make sense, provide drama and reader identification with the viewpoint character—and keep you on the straight plotting track.

Remember you *never* have to change viewpoint in order to write a novel that will sell. Get yourself thoroughly grounded in the fundamentals before you try to test the harder variations! You may find that you like basic scene structure so much that you will never want to try a variation.

Also, you should not be discouraged to realize that there are variations to the lovely bedrock structure of scene and sequel. That fact only holds out additional promise to you. Learn the basic way, and know you can build a career on it. Know that you have more growing you can do later, when you're truly sure of yourself and already on the road to commercial success. But be glad to know that basic scene-sequel structure is enough in itself, provided that you learn to do it well.

By way of proof that great success can be achieved with single viewpoint, consider best-selling novelist John Grisham. After scoring high with a number of novels in which there were multiple viewpoints—although viewpoint changes seldom, if ever, took place within a given scene—he hit the number one spot on the best-seller list in 1995 with *The Rainmaker*, a long, complex story told entirely from a single viewpoint narrated in first person.

If study of this chapter requires review for a week or more, and the suggested work takes even a bit longer, I hope you won't grow the least bit discouraged. The harder you work, the more you can learn. The more you learn, the sooner you'll start to sell.

So get to work!

Chapter Ten

Setting and Mood

As contemporary readers of the novel become more and more selective, the ambitious writer needs more tools in his arsenal in order to attract a wide audience. Increasingly, the novel's setting is a major factor.

In the past, novelists sometimes could get away with a somewhat predictable setting for their story. But today, readers demand more vivid sense impressions, more factual information and better interaction between character, motivation and the story locale. The growing popularity of the so-called "regional novel"—a book set in a somewhat unusual setting, such as John Grisham's books that take place in Memphis or Jean Hager's cozy mysteries set at a bed-and-breakfast in a small town in Arkansas—makes accurate and vivid description of locale even more important to the reader, who probably has never been in those places.

In the classic mysteries of Ross McDonald set in the decaying urban sprawl of southern California, the look and sound and sense of the area permeate every chapter. The *feel* of those often shabby motels and cafes, growing out of the author's precise descriptions of them, also makes the storyline more credible.

More recently, Tony Hillerman has achieved great success with his books set in the American Southwest and embedded in the Native American culture. And Eve K. Sandstrom has been well rewarded for her "Down Home" mysteries, which flourish in a unique, hot, dusty, small-town Oklahoma that she portrays well.

The general fiction reader wants to be drawn into an imaginary world and be entertained there. To draw the reader in, the writer has to provide good description of what the story place looks like, sounds like, possibly smells like—and feels like.

Thus, a writer who wants to present an effective story must take story setting very seriously. But what's actually involved in this task?

1. You must *select your setting carefully.*
2. You must *learn to know your setting intimately.*
3. You must *make sure it's presented vividly.*

Let's look at each of these factors.

SELECTION

Sometimes a setting seems to be picked almost by accident or as an afterthought. This mistake can doom an otherwise salable story. The setting must not only be believable, it must mesh properly with the plot and characters.

It's hard to imagine, for example, that a lighthearted, cozy mystery involving the theft of a prize-winning quilt could be played out successfully against the backdrop of a bleak and gritty city slum. The elements would not match up: The grim setting would destroy the desired light tone of the story at every step, and it would be almost impossible to get anyone to believe the quilt plot in that setting anyway. In a similar way, the historical romance could hardly work for the reader if the writer did not provide minute details of the dress and living conditions of the era portrayed.

Therefore, in evaluating a setting, certain practical questions of credibility must be asked:

1. Is it believable that the desired plot would take place in the setting under consideration?
2. Is it believable that this setting would have in it the kind of people I need to make this plot work?
3. Will descriptions of this setting contribute to the kind of emotional mood I want to evoke in the reader?

Our real lives may be jarred now and then by news reports of big-city–type gang violence in a small rural community, or a small-town policeman solving a case by using the very latest DNA test, or a sunny oceanfront community's atmosphere that is somehow bleak and miserable. Such things can happen.

In the world of fiction, however, events, people and mood should usually be tailored in a way to *fit*, not detract from, one another. Thus, a plot concerning gang violence would be more believable, and have more impact, if set in an inner city environment; an officer with the savvy to use modern DNA testing would be much more credible if placed in a metropolitan center; and a mood of bleakness and despair would be more convincing in a hostile, dirty town in the middle of a harsh winter. And if you plan to write a romantic historical novel set in Elizabethan England, your chances probably will be better if you set it in some place where you can have castles and carriages and dark forests to use as mood-enhancing backdrops.

KNOWING THE SETTING WELL
It's not enough, however, to choose the right setting. The next step is to get to know that setting as intimately as possible.

No one can guess all the facts about the story's physical world. But here are some of the things that almost always must be known.

- The climate at the time of year to be used.
- Details of the look of things—from terrain to buildings to quality of streets to how the residents ordinarily dress. (And if there is a particular real-life building or lake or mountain involved, exactly what the appearance or construction or depth or height of that thing really is.)
- How the place sounds—traffic noises, noon whistles, whisper of wind through trees, foghorns in the bay, coyotes howling in the night.
- How the place smells, if that's a factor—and in a town near an oil refinery or a pulp mill, it may be.
- How the place feels—whether it seems generally happy or gloomy or isolated or open or whatever.
- Population density—whether a street or road should be crowded or empty; whether a walk down the sidewalk in the evening means loneliness or being pushed around in a crowd; whether the office is spacious and isolated from the next, or is a cramped cubicle separated from its neighbor only by a six-foot metal partition.

- Quality of light—whether it's usually sunny or gloomy, or if a high hill makes sunset come prematurely, or if the office has bright windows or solid walls and blue-tinged overhead lights.

This suggestive list provides an idea of directions you should take in your own research.

Learning the answers may not always be easy. But a good writer will never *guess* what a town looks like, how the inside of a bank appears or what color best describes the lake. The good writer will *find out,* either by going there (the best), by looking up information in the library, by interviewing someone who knows the answers or a combination of all three. A single mistake in presentation of a physical setting will be caught by somebody. Count on that. And for that person who caught the error, all belief in the story is lost.

Unfortunately, editors are very smart and check everything. They are usually the ones who spot the mistake—and back goes the manuscript, rejected.

Of course some settings will be entirely fictional. But that doesn't mean anything goes. If the setting is not a real, specific place, it at least is in a region of a country or some identifiable part of the world. Your story's Montana town in the northern Rockies may have a brief snowstorm in May or June, for example, and that's acceptable because real Montana mountain towns do have late snows sometimes. But a writer couldn't put that same June snowstorm in Florida and then beg off by arguing that "It's not a real town! I made it up!"

The moral: When in doubt, check it out. Thoroughly.

VIVID PRESENTATION
Once the details have been found and checked and double-checked, a big piece of setting work is done. *How* the setting will be presented is another question, however.

Ordinarily we think of description as a sentence or paragraph, or several paragraphs, which describe the physical attributes of a place in a kind of stop-action technique. This kind of static description, whether from an omniscient viewpoint or the viewpoint of a character, is good and necessary.

In writing descriptions, you should strive for strong, accurate nouns and active verbs. Color and contrast often are a key to describing something visually. Short sentences are better than long ones, and a heavy reliance on adjectives or adverbs is probably a signal that the description is going on too long or limping. Static description often takes a very careful rewrite to make it as pointed and vivid as possible.

Sometimes, however, especially in fast-paced novels, static description is not practical. The action gets going pretty fast, and the last thing we want to do is slow the reader's pace— which static description tends to do. In such cases it might be deadly to stop to describe something about the setting, because, after all, when we stop to describe, we *stop*. Plot development, character movement, thought, dialogue—all come to a halt while the description is rendered. For this reason, it's wise to consider putting some of the description of the setting into *glimpses on the fly*.

In this technique, the writer does not "back off" to describe anything, but stays firmly in the viewpoint of the lead character. Then, as that character continues to talk, or drive the car or run down the street, she has only enough story time to get a glimpse of this, hear a bit of sound there, perhaps catch a whiff of pine tree as she hurries past the park.

This kind of description on the fly must be planned carefully, with information sprinkled through the character's movement in very small, selective bits. A general rule is that even a simple description—of a building, say, or the view from the side of the mountain—must be broken into several small compartments of information and inserted a bit at a time.

Remember two things: You must stay solidly in viewpoint for description on the fly, and your viewpoint character in motion *does not have time* to take in more than fleeting impressions. For example, a young woman fleeing a stalker on foot through the city streets might glance back and spot him rushing through the dense sidewalk crowds behind her; then later look up with dismay at the clotted traffic blocking her way across the busy intersection just ahead; then—again later—hear the noon chimes of the clock tower as she runs down the side street; then (after more chase details) feel the first spatter of warm summer rain on her face as she gets to the next corner; then (later still) smell Karmelkorn at a red-and-white plywood booth across the way. But she would not have time to get a full impression of any of these things, so you would have to present them fast, in a fragmentary form.

Such glimpsed details can accomplish as much as a longer view in keeping the reader aware of the looks and smells and feel of the city setting, while at the same time keeping the plot on the boil.

A fine exercise—one you should undertake often—is to pause a moment wherever you are, look around, listen, and then imagine how you would describe this place and time in several paragraphs, from a relaxed storytelling posture, as opposed to how you might move a character through it, describing vivid highlights on the fly.

Having done this, you should get back to your word processor or work journal as soon as possible and *write* those descriptions.

Such exercises have several benefits. They make you observe your world more closely, which can make you a better writer generally. They also test and strengthen your selection of words and scenic details. And they teach you to produce sharper, shorter, harder-hitting descriptions of setting when you are working to show your reader things about the world in your novel.

As usual, I can't force you to do this work. All I can say is that it's useful. I hope you'll take it from there.

HANDLING FACTUAL INFORMATION
Setting can be more than physical description, of course. That's often the most vital aspect; however, there is also the matter of *factual information* about a novel's setting, and sometimes that can be crucial too.

Ordinarily, we tend to focus on current factual information, such data as the following:

- Geographical or topographical details. Mountain scenery or plains? Hot southern summer or the milder summer of Canada?
- The town's population, form of government, biggest building, major business.
- Kinds of plants and animals that may be seen.
- Special techniques or information that may be known or

used by the main character—what he needs to know if he is a CPA, for example, as opposed to his special factual expertise if he happens to be a farmer.

Every story setting will dictate its own list of needed factual information to make it seem real.

Presentation of setting facts can be handled in much the same way as descriptions of sensory details. Here, however, "dumping in" great gobs at a time is even more dangerous than it is with description. The careful writer finds ways to slip in short paragraphs of setting facts that the reader must know. But she will also develop brief scenes in which the information can be brought out by the characters themselves.

This is done by creating a felt need in the viewpoint character to learn certain facts about the environment. You set things up so your character needs to know something. Then you have this character ask one or more other story characters about the needed information. Maybe you can fix it so that the would-be informant isn't very eager to talk, so your viewpoint character has to work hard to pry the information out of him—thus making up a dramatic scene. As the other story person tells the viewpoint character what she needs to know, the reader learns it also.

In all of this, a credible story world will slowly be built up, one that should convince the reader and transport him into the story's setting.

ALL THE INTANGIBLES

In terms of total credibility, however, today's markets demand that you know and deal with other aspects of setting as well. I call these *setting intangibles*.

Here we are talking about such matters as *historical* setting, *cultural* setting and *national* or *regional* setting. And we can get into some deep water when we work with these factors.

Your plot has to fit your setting. Your characters have to fit both. The historical, cultural and regional orientation of a setting can directly affect how people there think and live.

If you think of genre fiction—the western, for example— the truth about plot fitting with setting is immediately obvious. The traditional western simply cannot take place in New

York City in 1996. A novel aimed at the contemporary romance market won't likely succeed if you set it in a ghastly slum in Hong Kong in 1922. You're going to have some trouble making you reader believe several characters' preoccupation with the battle of Shiloh if you set them in a small town in the Klondike where they have always lived.

Other examples that come to mind are not so extreme. In Detroit not so long ago, on the night before Halloween, kids celebrated "Devil's Night," traditionally a night for pranks, by doing everything from soaping car windows to (sadly!) burning abandoned buildings. In not-so-far-away Columbus, Ohio, meanwhile, children went door to door in costumes asking for candy, as part of that city's "Beggars' Night" tradition. In isolated farm homes across much of America, they didn't do anything at all outside the home that night, but perhaps bobbed for apples or made fudge.

In each case, if you had asked the locals why they were doing what they were doing, they would have blurted, "Because that's what we do here."

It would be a very wise answer. Tradition varies with place, or setting, just as attitudes, fears, hopes, beliefs, expectations and all things do. If you set a story in San Francisco, that fact alone sets up a historical-cultural backdrop radically different from a setting somewhere in Utah.

TIME SETTING

Sometimes the place may not be as important in determining plot or character motives as the *time*. The writer who sets a novel in the New York City of 1918 is *not* dealing with the same environment that would exist in a novel set there today. On the very simplest level, the 1918 characters would not have such things as faxes, cell phones, car radios, TVs, or probably even a car. At a deeper level, your character of 1918 would be preoccupied with, and concerned about, far different problems than would your contemporary character. This would have an impact on your character's attitudes and assumptions about almost everything, which would make his motivation quite different.

So if plot, character and setting are to be in total, credible harmony, we must think of the setting's historical background, region and culture, too.

CULTURAL CONSIDERATIONS

At the outset we mentioned two contemporary mystery novelists, Eve K. Sandstrom and Tony Hillerman. They both work on the current scene. But their stories feel and are vastly different because of the settings they employ. It's not just that Sandstrom's southwestern Oklahoma town is out on the dusty prairie flats, while Hillerman's people live in the desert with mountains close by.

It's the part of the story settings related to history and prevailing culture that makes the mysteries profoundly different. Oklahoma was settled late, mostly by southerners, and attitudes are mostly southern to this day. Hillerman's area around Shiprock has been Indian land for longer than anyone knows, and its history is filled with ancient Native American tradition; therefore, the people act differently.

A characteristic Sandstrom mystery plot simply would not work in a Hillerman setting, and vice versa, not because the places look different, but because the "intangibles" such as history and culture have bred far different people.

There is much more to be concerned with when we use the simple term "setting." When you feel the need for considerably more discussion on this topic, you may wish to refer to my book on the subject (*Setting*, Writer's Digest Books) mentioned earlier. For now, a reminder of the points we've discussed should get you well on your way to improved handling of setting.

KEY POINTS ON SETTING

Remember that selection of setting is probably far more important than you may have suspected.

- Pick a setting that will help make your story more believable.
- Carefully mix and match setting with other story elements such as plot and characters.
- Do whatever is necessary to get to know the selected setting intimately.
- Learn the most effective ways to present details of your setting.

- Be alert to the often-overlooked intangible effects of setting.

It sounds like a lot of work, and sometimes it is. But thought beforehand, good research and artful presentation can make all the difference between a near miss and a sure sale.

ANALYSIS ASSIGNMENT

Set aside time for some more analytical work over the next few days. Go back over two or three of those favorite (and already marked-up) novels of yours. Search out passages, sentences, or even fragments that identify the setting as to place and time. How "lush" is the description? Why? How does the character motivation mesh with the setting's cultural, regional or historical details? Does the writer usually describe a little or a lot? In static description or "on the fly"?

When you begin to have answers to these and other questions that will occur to you, take your analysis a step farther. Ask yourself *why*—why the description is lush, if it is, or why it's terse; why the author puts factual information in where and when she does; why some detail of the setting helps you believe the motives of some character.

It's seldom good form to put an "etc." on the end of a sentence, but I was mightily tempted at the end of the last one. You should be able to come up with more angles of observation than I've suggested and a lot more questions *why*. Have you done so? If you haven't, maybe you're being lazy without realizing it.

And finally—have you already begun writing notes and conclusions about setting in your work journal? If you haven't, you have not yet begun to anchor the things you're learning in words that mean the most to you—your own. Sometimes it hurts, this forcing yourself to log positive conclusions. But it clears your thinking and makes a permanent record.

(How he does nag!) But it really is important.

Chapter Eleven

Handling Story Time

An odd fact often becomes apparent to the novelist about the time his first book is published: There is no relationship between the time he takes to write a story and the time it may take a reader to read it. Once, after spending many months of intense labor on a relatively short novel, I saw this fact most clearly when I read the first review. It said something like:

"This is an enjoyable two-evening read, with lots of suspense."

"Wait a minute!" I thought in distress. "That makes it sound like I *wrote* the thing in a couple of evenings."

So it's true that the amount of time you spend working on a book will have no direct impact on how much time the reader may invest in reading it. (It may even be that any remote relationship is inversely proportional: The longer you work on the yarn, the more gripping it will be, and so the faster it will read.)

It's sort of discouraging, and the source of an additional problem for the writer: You must always try to be aware of the *reader's* sense of pace and time, not your own. Or to put it another way, you must never be confused by the amount of time you may put in creating a scene or chapter, because writer time is invisible to the reader; if you start thinking that your segment that took a long time to write will take a long time to read, then the pacing of your novel may get all out of whack because that feeling may have no relationship to how much time it actually takes the reader to read it—or how fast or slow time may seem to go for the reader during that reading.

You may, for example, labor mightily for two or three days on revision of a transitional page of copy which is supposed to give the reader the sense of a month's time passing in the narrative. Then, because you have invested a lot of time in the creation, you assume the reader will be slowed down to read your deathless prose and get the desired sense of narrative time going by. But if you then look at your passage coldly and calculate what's going on in terms of time, you may come up with something like this:

STORY TIME = one month.
WRITER TIME = three days.
READER TIME = two minutes.

What to do? Awareness of the phenomenon is the critical factor. Once you see clearly that there's no necessary relationship between the times, you can discard entirely any awareness of how long it took you to create a segment; that's an author problem that nobody else cares about. With that false feeling out the window, you can then try to manipulate the reader's feeling about time to coincide with the amount of time going by within the story.

This is important. If the reader is allowed to read a mile a minute through your segment intended to show the passing of a year in story time, the disparity between reading time and story time may detract from his total belief in the story at that point. On the other hand, if you want to portray a tight, fast-moving sequence of events occurring in a very brief time span, but write it in such a way that the reader is slowed to a snail's pace in his reading—taking thirty minutes, for example, to read about a two-minute fight—then again a credibility gap will open in the story at that juncture.

So handling story time and reader awareness of same is vital, and you can do it in two ways. The first is through awareness and manipulation of basic narrative principles I have already alluded to in chapter nine, Scene and Sequel. Let's review and elaborate on what we learned there about timing.

CONTROLLING PACE THROUGH STRUCTURE

Here are the general principles to bear in mind:

The more intense the pressure, the more slowly and

minutely you cover the action or thought, moment by moment, with nothing left out. These high points, then, may represent only minutes in story time, but, ironically, may require *more reader time* than the passage of a year somewhere else in the story.

To put this another way, the bigger the scene, the longer it is likely to be, and therefore the longer the time the reader will have to invest in getting through it.

But here's a paradox. When conflict is happening (a scene), the reader reads faster and with more total absorption. Therefore, the long sequence, which may require a lot of reader time, may *seem* to the reader to go at lightning speed, and may *seem* to require little time at all to get through.

The moral: You can't count pages and assume that a ten-page segment will necessarily *feel* longer (and therefore slower) than another passage that might be only two pages in length. It's content and structure that control reader feeling about story time, not length.

Moments of meditation and review (sequel) tend to read more slowly. Therefore, even a relatively short sequel passage may give the reader the effect of slowing down, passing a lot of time.

Conclusion: You can control the pace of your novel in large part by juggling of scene and sequel. Even the longest scene reads swiftly and seems to rush along in little reader time. Even a brief sequel slows her down, relaxes some of her tensions—and gives the impression of more of her (reader) time passing.

If your story is going too slowly: Build your scenes and shorten your sequels. If your story is going too swiftly and thoughtlessly: Trim your scenes and/or build up your sequels.

This is the key to giving your novel "peaks and valleys." I heard about peaks and valleys from English professors for years and never could find the damned things. That's because it makes no more sense to speak of peaks and valleys in fiction than it does to say a story has a beginning, a middle and an end. What does *that* mean? So does a Dachshund!

What we're really talking about when we mention peaks and valleys is the manipulation of story pace by the author. Fiction readers can get dulled by pace that never changes.

Thus, in an action-packed story, it's necessary to insert quieter, slower-paced segments now and then so that the faster parts won't just seem to run all together in a blur. In a slow novel of character, on the other hand, it may be necessary to insert some faster-moving scenes here and there to help keep the reader excited and alert.

You manipulate reader time for dramatic purposes and to reflect in the most general way the time scheme of the novel. So, as more briefly mentioned in chapter nine, you have to do more in plotting than string out equal-length scenes and sequels. When you need the story to fly along and seem to take no time at all to read, you intensify and lengthen your scenes, and possibly truncate or even eliminate some sequels that would tend to slow things down. Conversely, when you feel the need to slow the pace, you lengthen your sequels.

CONTROLLING PACE WITH MODE OF DISCOURSE
Another way of controlling the speed of your novel is through the various *modes of discourse* you might use in any given passage. Let's look at them and note their characteristics.

Dramatic Summary
This is the fastest moving of the modes. Here the writer tells what's happening in somewhat condensed form, often sharply summarized and with time gaps, just as economically as she can write it. The passage whizzes along at breakneck speed—rushes the reader forward with the impression of practically no time (for the reader) passing.

Example:

> I left the office, hurried down the stairs and got behind the wheel of the car. Moments later I hit the turnpike and put the accelerator to the floor, the big engine whining, the speedometer climbing toward one hundred. I reached Joplin at noon, St. Louis less than four hours later—confronted Slade in his office at six.

Dramatic summary is used when speedy transition between scenes is needed, when the writer wants to hurry the story along, or when something dramatic is happening that doesn't lend itself to scene structure. When you write dramatic summary, your artistic "distance" from the story may be considerable and you may even get out of viewpoint, lapsing into an almost objective observer style. This can be dangerous in terms of continued reader identification with the major character, but the pace is incredible.

It's a mode of discourse to be used, with care, when picking up the plot pace and reader sense of speedy time passage are essential.

Dramatic Action

Next to swiftest, this is the stuff of scene—give and take, stimulus and response, action onstage *now*, with no summary. A brief example:

> I stepped into the dark room. Couldn't see a thing. Heard the slightest rustle of movement somewhere near the desk and knew he was here. I slid along the wall to my right. *Get behind him*, I thought. My foot touched something and betrayed my movement and there was a bright orange burst of light across the room and a simultaneous deafening crash and something slammed into my shoulder, knocking me backward with shocking impact. Pain filled me. I heard him coming around the desk. Desperate, I rolled. . . .

Whether you are in such violent physical confrontation in your scene, a dialogue argument or something much quieter, the intensity level is much the same. Lots of reader time may be devoted to the minute examination of every instant of story time, but the effect is involvement plus speed, speed, speed.

Dialogue

Dialogue is often the stuff of scene, too. It's story speech, told stimulus and response, with no summary. It, too, goes like gangbusters, but affects the reader as slightly slower and less manic than dramatic action.

Example:

> Mary felt a desperate need to talk about something— anything—to try to ease the tension.
> "What time is it?" she asked.

"Three o'clock," Nan said.

"And he's supposed to arrive at what time, did you say?"

"Now. Right now." Nan's voice cracked. "You know that as well as I do!"

So much for talk, Mary thought. "Sorry."

"Just shut up, that's all."

There will be more about dialogue later, especially in chapter fourteen. For now, just note that it's involving and quite fast-moving.

Narration

On the surface, narration looks a bit like dramatic summary. But it deals with more important events, and so is much more detailed. There can also be summary or condensation here, but because so many more details are provided, the effect is of much slower pace. Narration tends to involve long passages, so I won't quote one here. But we'll take a long look at this mode, too, in chapter fourteen.

Description

This mode orients the reader to the story world, whether the description is of setting, another character's appearance or expression, or even of the viewpoint's internal workings. The key point is that description *stops or sharply slows the action* in order to take its look.

Example:

She was tall, willowy, with legs he would remember forever. The sun backlit her pale hair, making a golden halo around her as she walked toward him. Her sky-blue sundress bared honey-colored shoulders and arms. Except for tiny earrings she was innocent of jewelry. Her wide hazel eyes already looked puzzled, even hurt, as he reached toward her.

Although there is a modicum of action here, the general effect is of very little happening—little forward story movement. And when little seems to be happening, the story creeps or stands still, and reader time seems to slow, even to drag.

So pure description, or even a variation which allows slight movement during an essentially descriptive passage, will make reader time pass and slow everything down.

Exposition

Slowest of the modes, exposition is the advancement of straight factual information. Some is essential in every novel. Example:

> Joe was 34. He was born in Dallas. He moved to New York after college at SMU. After working three years in a hotel on Park Avenue South, he met a wealthy widow and won her affections sufficiently so that he would never have to work again. He liked big cars. She bought them for him. He spent his afternoons playing bridge.
>
> Bridge is a card game that grew out of a British pastime called whist. Four play in partnerships against one another. The entire pack of 52 cards is used. . . .

You will note that this passage moves more clearly into pure exposition with the second paragraph. The first includes elements of dramatic summary. Such a mixture of modes is commonplace. Even so, the effect is to slow the reader down . . . make him feel like story time has slowed or stopped, too.

TIME OUT FOR WORK

Several of the modes of discourse described briefly in this chapter are given more detailed discussion elsewhere in this book. A later chapter is devoted solely to two of the most important, dialogue and narration. Description, too, has already fallen under scrutiny in chapter ten, as a vital part of setting. As you think about these timing devices, you will probably see other connections to other techniques. I hope you'll take the time to look for these connections because the search will enhance your growing sense of how all storytelling techniques dovetail with one another.

In addition, it's clearly to your benefit to be able to control story time and the reader's perception of it. Having read this chapter, you have the theory of how to do that. But as usual I want to urge you to do some work to test your understanding on a more practical level.

Select a chapter from a current novel. Go through the chapter meticulously and mark:

Dramatic summary in RED.
Dramatic action in ORANGE.
Dialogue in YELLOW.
Narration in BLACK.
Description in GREEN.
Exposition in BLUE.

Having done so, study the pattern of interplay between the modes. What is happening when each mode is used? What was the author's intent here? Do you sense your reactions as a reader speeding up or slowing down as you reread the passages?

What can you learn—and apply—from this analysis? Force yourself to log at least five positive conclusions in your work journal.

Additionally, you might make "the supreme sacrifice" I've urged on you at the end of other chapters. You might practice writing two or three brief sequences of your own in each mode. Or you might turn to some of the scene-sequel planning cards you outlined in chapter nine and consider how you might change them to speed up the pace or slow down the pace. Do you see a scene that might be put into dramatic summary for speed? A sequel that might be expanded to slow things down? A sequel that could be left out of your final draft for the sake of speed? Anything else?

Log your conclusions!

Chapter Twelve

Characters Make the Difference

A long time ago in his book *Writing: Advice and Devices,* Walter S. Campbell said there were eight ways to present a character in fiction:

1. By action of the character
2. By speech of the character
3. By effect of the character on other story people
4. By the character's reactions to other story people and circumstances
5. By what other story people say about the character
6. By explaining traits and motives of the character
7. By description of the character
8. By analyzing the psychological processes of the character

These observations are as true now as they were then. In this chapter we'll look at the processes involved.

Before getting to that point, however, another observation made in chapter three, in discussing the nature of story, seems eminently worth repeating as background for everything to follow: *Exaggeration is the first step toward creating vivid fictional characters.*

Time after time I have been confronted by new writers whose novels were peopled with characters who were flat, dull, unclear, uninspiring, uninteresting and plain old boring. Time after time I have confronted such writers with the bad news: "Your characters simply aren't interesting and realistic enough to engage a reader."

And sometimes—in the most extreme cases—the writer has looked shocked and replied, "But how can that be? These characters are all real people I know!"

This leads to the obvious conclusion about story people that I also mentioned earlier in this book: *Good characters are not real people; they are better than real people.*

Good characters are not only exaggerated, but more goal-oriented, more consistent (with tricks used to make them appear more complex than they really are), engaged in more dramatic circumstances than most of us ever encounter in day-to-day living, and more committed to their quest.

So in both this chapter and the next we'll look at some fundamental techniques and ideas that may help you build characters who are bigger and better than life. For nothing less will do. And if you detect a repetition of advice given earlier in other contexts, maybe you will get an insight into how every technique fits with every other—how the richly textured fabric becomes a whole.

EXAGGERATION OF PERSONALITY

An actual, real-life person, translated to paper as literally as possible, will look dull at best. Exaggeration is mandatory. Not only are appearances often exaggerated, but personality characteristics are, too. So the wise novelist makes the loyal character almost unbelievably loyal, the cruel character horribly cruel, the witty character outrageously brilliant and so on. Great fictional persons stand on the brink of caricature. And since they are so exaggerated and almost outrageous, the reader sees them through the veil of the reading process as lifelike.

Want a textbook example of exaggeration in character? Go back to the classics. There is no better teacher of this technique than Charles Dickens in his best works. Look, for example, at the vivid people walking through every page of *Great Expectations.*

If you happen to go too far in exaggerating in your own work, really making your story person "too much of a good thing," it is possible to tone down that character during revision. But if you err in the opposite direction and get far into your book with flat or insipid story people, it's usually much harder to beef them up. So as you write, it's wise to overstate your story people in the early going. You can always tone them down later if necessary, and chances are good that they may end up just right anyway.

Also, you may be delighted to learn that exaggerating your characters as you write about them tends to fire up your own imagination. The process is something of a mystery to me; I only know it happens: Start to write about a wild and crazy character, and she will begin to appeal to you, too, so that you see her even more vividly—and can make her even wilder.

Many years ago I was writing a western novel that worried me. Halfway through the book, its pace and my own interest seemed to be lagging. Having noticed (and logged the observation in my journal) that my interest in a novel often perked up when a new character came onstage, I decided to introduce a new story person solely for the purpose of adding zest to the tale.

Adding a major character more than halfway through a novel isn't recommended procedure, but I was desperate. So, throwing caution to the winds, I had my marshal riding along a ravine, hearing a great commotion on the far side of the hill, and looking to the hilltop to spy a clamorously exaggerated character.

He was well over six feet tall, that cowboy up there, astraddle a red roan horse and unsteady in the saddle. He was wearing red pants, a green shirt, a yellow vest, a blue ten-gallon hat, lizard boots with the rowels of his big silver spurs painted purple, and there were crossed shell belts over his chest. As my marshal stared in disbelief, the cowboy up there tumbled out of his saddle, and he and the horse rolled down the hill to crash to a halt in a dusty pile right at the marshal's feet.

An ordinary person would have been killed. But my new character jumped up laughing, and a pint bottle fell out of one of his back pockets. He was built like a wedge, with flaring wide ears, carrot-colored hair and an alarming gap in his face where two of his front teeth should have been. He had a big Colt strapped on, and a stick of dynamite in the top of one of his boots. *Nobody* had ever been like this guy.

After getting over my inbred English department embarrassment at having created such an exaggeration, I found myself chuckling at this weirdo. He started talking, and he was totally outrageous. My interest in him—and the novel—soared. It was a struggle the rest of the way to prevent him from taking over the story entirely.

I was still working as a student with Dwight V. Swain when this happened. I took pages of the novel to him for critique. I can still see him sitting up straighter behind his desk when my new character appeared . . . then beginning to read more intently, then starting to chuckle.

"Bickham," he chortled, slapping the pages with the back of his hand, "this is great. This is crude. Great barnbrush strokes. This *works*. We may get you over your experiences in the English Department yet!"

That novel sold. My character still fascinated me. I decided to try a comic western starring him. When I submitted *The Fighting Buckaroo* (written under my pseudonym, Jeff Clinton), Tom Dardis at Berkley Medallion wrote to accept the book for publication, and suggested a series about him!

That was how Wildcat O'Shea was born, and eventually he starred in fourteen novels. I still remember him with great fondness. No, he was not great literature. But he brought me— and a lot of readers—fun and pleasure. He also helped me buy a new house and put in a swimming pool. I tend to like characters who do things like that for me.

And all because I finally threw caution to the winds— stopped worrying about being corny or too crazy—and *really* exaggerated someone in a book.

No one can promise you a swimming pool, or even a rose garden, if you'll wildly exaggerate in characterizing too. But you may be amazed how well it works. Try it.

BUILDING UP A CHARACTER

Some other aspects of building up a story character are a little mysterious. The imagination works in wondrous ways, and every once in a while a character will just seem to blossom on the page for you without a lot of prior planning. Unfortunately, that doesn't happen often, and we can't build a professional career on mystery. Fortunately, on the other hand, there are a number of things about a story character that we can identify and work with in building a better character. So let's look at some of those.

THE NAME IS IMPORTANT

One of the first things the reader learns about a character, usually, is her name. The name can be important.

Sometimes we tend to grab a name for a major character out of the air, and fail to give it sufficient thought. But the name is sometimes the first way we begin to sense something about a character, and it's the single identity tag by which we will refer to her again and again and again.

What if we have a character named Mary Smith?

What happens if we change her name to Bubbles LaRue? Or Fifi? Or Sister Innocence?

Is there a difference implied *by the name alone* if we name a character Dirk Pitt? Or Percy Dovetonsils? Is an intrinsic difference in personality implied when we read names such as George Washington Jones or Tony DiRosario or Baron Rothschild or Billy Bob Tubbs?

The name itself may suggest character type, history or even ethnic background. So it's important to find the right one as your work on building the character proceeds in your mind.

In this connection, even the way you choose to refer to a character on subsequent reference may affect your reader's perception of him. After first telling the reader your character's name is John Blunt, will you later refer to him as "John Blunt" or "John" or "Blunt?"

The prevailing custom today is to refer to males by last name and females by first name. (Even in today's era of liberation and political correctness, to some readers it seems to sound "cold" when we speak of Mary Smith on second reference as "Smith." This trend is changing, but very, very slowly.) Conversely, referring to our character John Blunt as "John" on subsequent reference tends to warm the tone of the story and subtly soften the style, so that this first-name decision alone might make him somehow seem a softer character.

In a spy novel or suspense yarn, where the tone is generally cool anyway, characters almost always will be called by their last names only. In a romance, where the tone is intimate, the opposite might be true. But it's a fact that changing your method of reference to a character in this small way may alter the tone of your entire passage. Which only reinforces the point that your character's name may be immensely important in the reader's perception of that character.

PERSONAL HISTORY

In addition to knowing your character's name, of course, there are other things you need to know about her. One of the most important in many books is that character's *history*. How elaborately you devise a past for a character will depend on her role in the novel. A major character obviously needs more created past than a walk-on.

Depth of character-history planning can also depend on the type of person the character is. Even a fairly important character may not demand an elaborate personal history if he happens to be a grim, reticent, mysterious figure whose unknown past actually contributes to the sense of menace he radiates.

Even the type of story may affect how much history you need to invent for a character. In a romance novel, the checkered past of several characters may be explored at some length, while in a traditional western you may only need to know that the gunman had a hard life and once narrowly escaped hanging.

In the case of almost any major character, you should at least be able to fill out an imaginary job application. This *minimum* information should include:

- Name
- Date and place of birth
- Parents' names, ages, occupations, social status and present whereabouts
- Education
- Marital status and children, if any
- Military background, if any
- Health
- Job background
- Financial situation
- Awards, achievements of note, etc.
- Hobbies
- Favorite pastimes, such as favorite music, authors, sports events, entertainment personalities, etc.
- Ambitions.

I have a form in my computer for this data on characters. You may wish to devise one of your own. Some of the information may never enter the story *directly*. But forcing your imagination to build such a background for your character will stimulate further thought and bring out new ideas about her—and much of the information may enter the novel indirectly, in ways that surprise you. For the better you know your character, the more clearly you will tend to depict her.

GOAL CAN BE DEFINING

In addition, as we know by now after working a bit with the story question and scene structure, goal motivation is awfully important in storytelling. So it follows that a character to some degree will be defined by the goals he selects during the course of the novel. Someone once said, "Tell me what a person strives for, and I'll tell you what kind of person he is." Your study of the character's past, and how it leads to his present goal in the story, is vital.

The man who is almost violently driven to become governor of his state is quite a different sort than his neighbor who says all he wants in life is to be left alone. The woman whose goal is to be president of her law firm is different from her sister, who wants to find a good man, marry and settle down. The gold miner is different from the coal miner.

The moral here: The wise novelist is sure of what every character *wants* before she launches into writing about him.

THE SELF-CONCEPT

In chapter seven we looked at the self-concept of a person, and how preservation of that self-concept often provides the motivation for the person to pick a goal and strive for it. The self-concept, then, is obviously crucial to character definition.

To rephrase what was said earlier in this regard: Our most central goal is maintenance and enhancement of the symbolic self, or self-concept. Out of your character's background and present situation has come a view of herself which is consistent and precious to her. Somehow her story goal relates to that self-concept; the role she plays in her life and the novel does, too.

For *every* character who plays any significant role in your novel, you should have a sheet of paper or computer file that contains her statement: "I am _____," using your imagination to fill out her self-definition in a few words.

Having done this, you can clarify your thinking about the activities she takes part in—the things she does—which "plug into" and enhance her concept of herself.

As an example, one woman may say:

I am a businesswoman, and very efficient in what I do.

Her activities, therefore, may include working for a major oil company; writing a book about ways to improve employees' efficiency; dating a man whose work as an attorney she admires for his intelligence and power; driving a sleek British sedan because she admires the traditional British character; wearing business suits and practical shoes (but coolly feminine styles in the evenings); and living in a Manhattan apartment building used by upwardly mobile professional people.

Another character may say:

I am an outdoorsman and an athlete.

Aside from the fact that he works for the Forestry Service, wears flannel shirts and drives a Bronco, I'll let you imagine how his entire environment may be structured around roles that enhance his stated self-image.

Note also, however, that a character may often act the way he does, not only out of a positive self-concept, but also out of a *negative* one. By the process of accommodation, people often build a strength over what was once perceived as a weakness—real or imagined. How often have you seen a great athlete on TV in, say, the Olympics, and then heard the announcer tell how that marathon runner suffered polio as a child? How many fine public speakers once were terrified to face an audience, or even suffered a stutter or lisp? So sometimes a key to better understanding a character is to look for a lacking or weakness once perceived by the character as part of a hated self-concept, then struggled *against* in a battle that today results in activities and goals contrary to that old negative self-concept.

In real life you can easily find examples of people fighting to overcome old flaws they beheld in themselves as part of their self-concept—learning to play roles exactly the opposite of the weakness. In our recent history one need look no farther than a disabled person who became a great president despite being confined to a wheelchair, a wonderful jazz/popular pianist and vocalist who is blind, an NBA basketball player a full two feet shorter than many of his opponents, or an olympic gold medalist with asthma.

In a like manner, a person in real life—or a character in your novel—may to the present day harbor a bad self-concept, one he feels is unacceptable. So a man who defines himself as an opportunist or even a thief might try to convince himself that his background made him that way and there is nothing he can do about it. And he might act in harmony with a sick self-concept of this kind by taking unfair advantage of people, or stealing from them, because he considers himself that kind of person.

Thus self-definition can become a cornerstone of your characterization. As you become more aware of people in your everyday life, you will begin to hear them stating their self-concept in obvious ways you may have missed up until now. Note all the ways people tell you who and what they think they are. You will be amazed how consistent they are in acting exactly like the kind of person they define themselves to be.

Your journal should start to be sprinkled with specifics in this area. *Pay attention to how people talk about their self-concept.* Then make notes in the journal about it.

TRAITS AND TAGS

Another way of building story characters can be found in attention to personality *traits* and *tags*.

Personality traits in the broadest sense are those rather abstract descriptors of personality that you can name but seldom explain. A person is "strong," you say, or "sympathetic," or "nervous" or "overbearing."

Abstract words. Unconvincing. They paint no picture for the reader. And readers seldom believe what we as writers *tell* them; they want to be *shown*, and then allowed to draw their own conclusions about the story people, just as they observe people in real life and draw conclusions about them.

So it is not enough for you the author to know that Joan is nervous, compulsive, impatient and a little self-destructive. You have to devise a way to show these inner traits to the reader.

How? You hang tags on her.

A tag is simply an outwardly visible (or hearable) appearance or activity or habit or thing that you hang on the character, like a tag hanging on a piece of furniture, which says what the inner, abstractly named trait is.

Of course sometimes a tag is strictly a shorthand device to help the reader recognize a minor character, and this kind of tag may have little to do with personality. Your minor figure who works where the hero banks, for example, may wear pince-nez glasses and have a toupee that sometimes slips toward one ear. Or the mail carrier may limp, so that when we hear someone limp onto the porch, we know who it is. Such identification tags may not say much about underlying personality traits.

Major tags for major characters, on the other hand, not only identify people, they show something of what the person is like.

A personality tag is waved more often during the course of a novel than you might suspect. Readers forget. If, for example, you decide that one tag for "nervous Joan," mentioned just above, is that she smokes heavily, then in a 60,000-word novel you will probably show her smoking twenty or thirty times. In addition, you will devise *tag clusters* which all relate to her nervous smoking habit: You may show her asking for a light on four widely separated occasions; coughing six times; buying cigarettes twice; filling her lighter twice; opening a fresh pack three times; emptying an ashtray once; waving a hand with tobacco-stained fingers three or four times; and perhaps refusing to eat at some restaurant because it bans all smoking, saying, "I'm a smoker, that's all there is to it, and I'm too stubborn to be forced into quitting."

(Notice, incidentally, how she explains one aspect of her tag cluster—refusing the restaurant—by stating part of her self-concept.)

It may be that you will finally decide, on revision, that you waved a tag or tag cluster too often. You can always go back and delete a few. In my experience with new novelists, the opposite problem usually obtains: A good tag may be chosen, but then is wasted because it isn't shown nearly often enough. Good writers wave the tags often. How many times in *The Caine Mutiny* did Herman Wouk have Captain Queeg roll those steel balls around in his hand? How many times did Hamlet express his indecisive nature in poetry and action? How often in the old Star Trek series did Spock tell Captain Kirk, "It isn't logical" or some variation that revealed his nonemotional Vulcan personality trait? Only brainy Vicky Bliss, the star of Elizabeth Peters's mystery series, could talk so wisely and wittily about ancient history.

As with statements of self-concept, you don't have to look only in fiction to see tags at work. Many real-life people can be identified by obvious tags. Consider the following:

"Let me make this perfectly clear. I am not a crook."

A cigar, a round face, a bald head, a V-for-victory sign.

"Wow! Did you see him come in and boom! make that tackle?"

A mustache; a strut; a stiff-armed salute. *"Heil!"*

In case you had trouble, here's a footnote.[1]

Consider your friends, people at work, even those in your own close family. Can you see them exhibiting real-life tags that might say something about a personality trait? Write your observations in your journal, and don't just do this once: Plan to make it an ongoing practice for as long as you are a writer. You will harvest a gold mine.

Further, take time out to create tags for three or four characters of your invention. Identify a trait or traits in each, and set up tags to reveal those traits. Stretch your creativity. Have fun with this assignment while you learn.

HOW TO INTRODUCE A CHARACTER

In the following chapter we'll look at additional techniques for showing and deepening character. Here, however, it's time to take those aspects we already know and study tactical uses for them. How, for example, should you bring a character into your story? How do you show characters as consistent and recognizable after they've been offstage for a while?

The single most important moment for a major character often is

---

1. In order: Richard Nixon; Winston Churchill; John Madden; Hitler.

when she first enters the story. Therefore it is vitally important to bring your majors on in the proper way. A weak or wrong first impression on the reader may never be remedied.

The most effective ways of introducing a character:

- Characteristic entry action
- Description of habitat
- Comment by other characters
- Direct author intrusion

Characteristic entry action is the most dramatic and most-used method. The door opens and in comes Marybell, doing and saying and acting and feeling and *being* absolutely characteristic. And with all her tags waving. She makes an instant and lasting impression. The reader feels she begins to know her at once.

So, for example, Marybell comes into your office. She keeps her eyes lowered, she sort of glides apologetically, she sits stiffly with knees pressed together tightly and nervously smooths her plain cotton dress; you notice she wears no polish on her bitten fingernails and that there is a little tic on the left side of her pale face.

Or, the next day, here comes the new, redesigned, customized, jet-propelled Marybell, the model for the new millennium. She knocks briskly and swings into the office, electric with energy, Italian pumps clicking sharply on the tiles. Her head is high, her hair is styled, she gives you a wide, confident grin and leans across your desk to shake hands, sits without hesitation in the proffered chair, crosses her legs, whips out a notebook and ballpoint pen, and fixes you with those keen, intelligent blue eyes that stare with total confidence.

In each example, you have already formed a sharp impression of Marybell from her characteristic entry action alone.

Sometimes your plans for plot in a novel will be subtly altered because—in order to bring on your character in characteristic action—you have to put in a scene that will have few downstream effects. In other words, sometimes you plot for character. So maybe you have to introduce Jimmy the Pilot during a plotted airline emergency to introduce him in a way that will show his daring, coolness and resourcefulness. Or possibly you have to show Jennifer talking long-distance to her aged mother to introduce her in an action that best demonstrates her characteristic kindness and devotion to her family.

WORK ON YOUR OWN NOVEL

Stop now.

Think about a major character in your novel.

If you could first introduce him onstage anywhere, at any time, doing and saying *anything*, in order to give him a smashing entrance:

Where would you have him?
What would he be doing?
How?
What tags would be waving?
What would be his overwhelming *dominant impression*?

Write it!

THE NEED FOR OTHER METHODS OF INTRODUCTION

You can see, then, how characteristic entry action is a great way to bring on a character. But it's unlikely that you want to bring on every character this way, because your reader may begin to figure out what you're doing—detect the pattern behind your strategy. You don't want that to happen; when the reader figures out your pattern or usual tactic, she's likely to begin to consider your novel "predictable" or even dull.

Also, there can be problems sometimes with characteristic entry action, despite its power. For one thing, you as a writer face the task of naming and identifying and describing the new character at the same time she is talking and acting, at the same time another character is reacting, at the same time you're trying to keep plot moving, at the same time Marybell is still coming on like gangbusters, at the same time—well, you get the idea. Introducing a character in motion can be hard because so many other things tend to require attention at the same time.

In addition, if you plot a great many scenes to provide perfect character entries, you might end up with so much action for plot that you could find yourself on page eighty before the real story gets much of a start.

Good thing there are other methods for backup.

INTRODUCTION BY HABITAT

The technique of introducing a character by first showing his *characteristic habitat* is useful and often used. It was one of the favorites employed time and again by novelist Harold Robbins, and you can often see it at work in books by writers as diverse as Jack Higgins and Phyllis Whitney.

In this stratagem, before the character enters the scene directly, you describe his office or his car or his apartment or his clothes closet or his country club—whatever may tell the reader much about the roles the character plays, the kind of environment he has chosen or built around himself to enhance his self-concept—the habitat which says indirectly who and what he is.

An example off the top of my head:

The office on the top floor of the forty-story bank building reeked of power. Its glass wall looked out over the heart of the financial district. Heavy carpet masked sounds of work beyond the closed walnut door. On one interior wall: shelves of books that included works on finance as well as great literature. Another wall was dominated by a small but priceless Picasso. The big walnut desk was clean, efficient, graced by a marble pen-and-pencil set and a framed picture of Harrigan himself with his beautiful young wife and their two children, whom he adored. Hidden in the bottom drawer on the right-hand side of the desk was a booklet he had ordered and received only recently; it described many ways by which a man who was terminally ill might take his own life.

After such a static description of habitat—which might extend a bit longer than this little sample—we can have character Harrigan enter the habitat. And we already know a great deal about him.

The only grave danger in introduction by habitat is the fact that it usually involves static description. And you will remember that description is one of the slower modes of discourse.

COMMENT BY OTHER CHARACTERS

Another method of character introduction is the employment of *comment by other characters*.

Here you simply set up a scene in which one character already introduced wants to know about the character you plan to bring on next. Use Harrigan as an example again, and suppose we know nothing about him. Have previously-introduced Donna and Dave meet somewhere. Donna says, "Harrigan is due to arrive today." Dave says, "I don't know a thing about him. What can you tell me?" Then the two have a conversation in which one character asks questions and the other tells what you, the author, want the reader to know.

Having accomplished this method of introducing data to the reader, almost like the chorus of ancient Greek theater commented on the action for the audience, you can bring Harrigan onstage to a reader well-prepared for his arrival.

DIRECT AUTHOR INTRUSION

Finally, you may sometimes introduce a character by *direct author intrusion*. One novelist who uses this technique a lot is Sidney Sheldon. The writer begins a new segment of his story by simply dumping in factual data about the new character. Or he may vary this approach slightly by writing a personality description that is close in style and intent to the old Greek "characters" by such authors as Theophrastus, from whose ancient work a modern book has been prepared. In *The Characters of Theophrastus*, J.M. Edmonds suggests that Theophrastus writes short descriptions of characters by *type*—"the glutton," "the coward," etc. But there is no reason why you can't use the same approach to introduce a character by name rather than personality type.

Again, there are dangers in use of this device. One is similar to the speed problem cited in connection with use of habitat. Introduction by intrusion tends to be factual—straight exposition. And you will remember that exposition is the slowest of all modes of discourse. So your story pace will slow every time you use this technique.

In addition, you must be very careful to present direct factual material of this kind as unobtrusively as possible. You're often out of any character's viewpoint when you use this technique, and you can't let the reader start hearing "your" authorial voice. You can't give some opinion about what the reader should decide about the character being introduced, for example, and you can't let an "I"—meaning you, the author—slip in by accident.

Novelists sometimes skirt this potential danger—that of the author being *seen* as intruding—by having a viewpoint character find a document or computer database or book that he can then read, getting the factual information in his viewpoint.

STUDYING PUBLISHED EXAMPLES

In your reading, try to be more alert to how characters are brought on. Note how good novelists use one device one time, another the next. Variety of approach enlivens the narrative, and as you grow as a novelist, you'll see that one approach may fit one character better than another—and that how you bring your people on will also affect your pace in the book.

ADDITIONAL POINTS TO REMEMBER

Beyond this—and before we begin to look deeper into the human personality and character development in the next chapter—a few additional points need to be remembered:

1. *Conflict creates character.* There is nothing like the pressure of a struggle—and the setbacks of scene endings—to bring out the true nature of your story person. Anyone can look good—or dull—when there is no pressure. Any time you are having trouble with a character, it may well be that you are not making life difficult enough for him.

2. *Character is defined by action.*

3. *Internalizations can mean a lot.* The true nature of a character can often be revealed through the judicious use of the *internalizations* that are an integral part of stimulus-response transactions. Make the stimulus-response transaction complex by making the stimulus tough or unexpected, and your character will be driven into an internalization before being able to respond. This gives you the chance to show how she thinks and feels—and so to characterize her briefly. Having done this dozens of times in the course of a novel, eventually you will have slipped in a tremendous amount of information about her.

4. *Other characters define characters.* If you have set up a sympathetic character named Archibald, and he tells someone else

that he would go to the wall for Biff, "a really great guy," then the reader will tend to believe Biff is a great guy before ever meeting him.

In fiction, good people tend to like good people, and bad tend to like bad, and never the twain shall meet—except in conflict. Don't hesitate to let your story people characterize one another in conversation with others.

5. *Your character can speak for himself.* Given half a chance, your character will tell the world the kind of person he is. As we discussed earlier, people in real life—and in fiction—often explain their behaviors by saying, "I didn't steal the money, because I'm an honest man." Or "Basically, I'm a sentimental jerk, but at least I'm honest."

So don't be afraid to have your characters talk about themselves in this way. And please also note that sometimes you can create scenes in which two characters argue about one's view of the other—or about one's view of herself!

I don't think I'll elaborate on that. But I hope you think about it. It's a very useful device and one very much in tune with the reality of how we function in real life.

CHARACTERISTIC PREOCCUPATION

Finally, chew on this one for a while: *Every major character has a characteristic preoccupation.* So, too, do most goal-motivated people in real life. The businessman tends to be preoccupied with improving and selling his product. The lawyer tends to be preoccupied with her current case in court. The sick person is preoccupied with trying to get well—and possibly with fear of death.

These preoccupations have to do with real life or story plot, circumstance, time and place. And equally with background, felt needs and perceived lackings in the self-concept, story goal—virtually everything we've discussed.

Think about your major viewpoint character. What is her characteristic preoccupation, the thing that worries her most often, the problem or goal that comes back into her mind every time it can? To what worry or goal or sadness or hope does she tend to relate almost anything she encounters?

It might be possible to write an entire instructional book

about characteristic preoccupation as a technique in the novel. The character with a strongly perceived characteristic preoccupation will act certain ways, think certain ways and feel certain ways because of that preoccupation. He will see all sorts of plot developments as relevant to his preoccupation, even if they have no actual relevance.

Just one example may clarify this. Suppose there is a sudden, unexpected snowstorm which dumps a foot of snow on the city's streets. For the man characteristically preoccupied with getting to work early every day to show his dedication, the traffic problem associated with the storm might instantly be perceived as *trouble getting to work on time.* Consequently he might become terribly nervous or angry, and vow, while waiting for the taxi, to buy a four-wheel-drive vehicle. But on the same street with Mr. Busy, his neighbor Carolyn might be characteristically preoccupied with physical fitness. She would look out the window and interpret the storm in light of *her* preoccupation, be delighted, and immediately get out the cross-country skis for a grand day of practice.

Same storm. Vastly different personal reactions and actions. Why? Different characteristic preoccupations.

If you handle characteristic preoccupation well, you can make your viewpoint character see almost any plot development as important; all you have to do is figure out how his preoccupation will *make* it relevant.

WORK TO BE DONE
For more practice—

Name some characters and write backgrounds for them.
Devise some traits and tags to match. Devise tag clusters.
Write a major background statement for at least one major character.
Write "job-application forms" for at least two others.
Take one of these characters and practice bringing her on in characteristic entry action. Through habitat. Through the other devices mentioned. See which works the best for you, and why.

Take your time on all this! If you press on before giving considerable time and thought to these matters, you're cheating yourself again.

If your imagination gets tired, don't quit and hurry into the next chapter of this book. Instead, sit down in an easy chair, relax, and think about the color green.

Then get back to work.

Chapter Thirteen

Making Story People More Interesting

I n the previous chapter we looked at several aspects of human nature and techniques the novelist can use to enhance reader understanding of fictional characters. Now we need to look a bit deeper into personality in order to find ways we might make our story characters even more interesting.

Some people understand those around them with a compassion, sensitivity and insight that amazes the rest of us. Fortunately, those of us who don't have such a gift can consciously learn to understand better, and then apply it to our work.

If you are one of those rare blessed ones who understands people almost at the level of instinct, I congratulate you. This chapter may offer very little that you don't already know. But if you are one of the vast majority who don't, perhaps something here can help you make your story characters more realistic-appearing—which is to say, more complex.

Real people—and the best characters in fiction—often act out of motives they understand vaguely, if at all. "That's just the way I am," they say, inadvertently referring to their self-concept. Or: "I've always been that way, it's my basic temperament." Which can refer to an entire school of psychology which looks not at *nurture*, as most psychology has tended to do since the time of Sigmund Freud, but at *nature*—traits of personality which may be programmed into the gene structure itself in ways we don't understand, or perhaps dictated in part by the uterine environment. Others may say, "I act as I act because my family has always acted that way," perhaps pre-consciously sensing the truths of Transactional Analysis and its emphasis on often-unexamined life scripts derived from parents, other family members, or even from cultural/ethnic/ national sources.

None of us can ever hope to understand it all. But the novelist can pick and choose and, out of even a superficial study, can come up with an eclectic approach to understanding human behavior that will help enormously in making his story people more complex. Let's begin by looking at some basic patterns of behavior that might help us in our work.

THE INTENTIONALLY DISHONEST CHARACTER

It's important to remember that the story character, just like people in real life, does not always have to tell the truth or reveal real motivations. So in your novel, your character may not always show her true feelings or thoughts because circumstances force her to be dishonest.

Such a dishonest character in your book does not necessarily have to be a person we dislike. Travis McGee, in the late John D. MacDonald's series, was often dishonest in the sense that he withheld information from people for good reasons, or in self-defense acted less intelligent and aware than he really was in order to fool people. McGee especially loved to play the innocent oaf with police, throwing them off the track so that they ignored him and thus left him alone to pursue his own investigations. Such dishonest ruses did not detract from his wide appeal, and indeed tended to make him appear more clever and admirable.

In a similar way, James Bond, hero of the "007" adventures written by Ian Fleming, seldom was entirely honest. His cool deceptions and outright dishonesty in dealing with his antagonists were crucial to his success in the high-stakes game of international spying. One classic example from *Goldfinger* is his deception of Goldfinger, tricking him into a high-stakes golf game. (That sequence, incidentally, is also a classic lesson in pure scene structure.)

Beyond such characters as these who lie and deceive by design—and *know* they are doing it—there are many more who deceive themselves as well as everyone else. That's because they simply cannot face their basic feelings.

Such characters—and people in real life—often display one or more of four basic behaviors which are most useful to the novelist. They're fairly easily understood on a mechanical level, and give us a place to start. We'll look at each in turn.

PROJECTION

A character may seem dishonest or puzzling because he is caught in the unrealized process of *projection*. This kind of person may be aware of some of his feelings and thoughts, but views his world unrealistically—and consequently acts dishonestly—because he projects his feelings onto others. His basic, unexamined assumption is, "All people feel as I do."

So the man with envy and thievery in his heart will assume that everyone else is the same, and will trust *no one*. He's likely to misconstrue the simplest well-meaning gesture as a maneuver to cheat or "get" him. Perhaps he'll have an elaborate burglar alarm system. On a more serious level, he may betray his best friend on the basis of a belief that good friends don't exist anyway—since he himself cares deeply for no one.

In romance, the woman madly in love with a man—even if he has shown no deep interest in her—may project her love onto him and truly believe he loves her as much as she loves him. Obviously, such a process sets her up for the most bitter and profound disappointment—and the man may *or may not* have done anything to encourage her delusions.

I once encountered a classic case of projection in real life. (Over the years I've witnessed many, just as you have.) It was a beautiful spring day and I happened to meet an acquaintance on Main Street.

"Good morning!" I said. "Beautiful day, isn't it?"

"How can you say that?" she cried. "You don't have to pretend for *me*!" And burst into tears.

Later I learned she had just lost someone very dear to her. So her day was not beautiful, as we met on the street; she had projected her misery onto the entire environment. And when I said it was a pretty day, she immediately assumed I was pretending—*because she was pretending* a calm she in no way really felt.

In engineering distrust, or setting up transactions between characters with a potential for disaster based on misunderstanding, you may find projection to be a useful device. For the character caught in such a process sees nothing clearly, and may be capable of anything that could grow out of his warped outlook on reality.

DENIAL

Another inaccurate way of looking at things involves the process of *denial*. Unfortunately, you see signs of this malady often in real life. The person in denial represses *totally* whatever feelings may be down inside somewhere.

Taught that anger is unacceptable to his parents, for example, a child may be faced with an intolerable conflict between his emotions and the demands of his parents, whom he loves. His feeling and showing of anger results in condemnation or rejection by his parents, or punishment. He learns quickly to feel bad about himself—his sense of self-worth suffers—when anger swells up inside him. So without conscious volition he learns a trick: to bury such unacceptable feelings so they are not allowed at all into his consciousness.

In one sense, this results in what we mean when we speak of "the unconscious." Part of this portion of personality is composed of feelings and thoughts that are simply too terrible (in reality or imagination) to be allowed into consciousness. They are still there, but we bury them—literally no longer know they exist.

And so our angry child grows up to become a man who can quite honestly (as far as he knows!) tell you: "I simply don't ever get angry. Anger is an emotion I never experience." So, even when faced in your story with ghastly wrongdoing against him or his loved ones, he feels nothing—and so does nothing in self-defense. Or a young girl senses potential rejection by her mother for experiencing the most innocent sexual stirrings, denies all such feelings—and grows up to be a cold and frigid wife. Or the youth denied of love, ridiculed as a sissy for showing love, or given no good examples of how to demonstrate love, may become an adult who feels no love for anyone, and whose behavior patterns border on those of the sociopath.

Use of denial in characters is often helpful to the novelist. If the denying character is placed in plot circumstances wherein the denial is tested again and again—and finally broken through—enormous amounts of energy may be liberated, and a character's life can be thrown into tumultuous upheaval as if at the click of a switch.

On a more superficial level, of course, we have all seen denial at work time and time again. We get into a discussion with a loved one, and the discussion becomes an argument. Our sister starts shouting, and her face gets red; she is shaking all over.

"Don't get angry about it," we say.

"Angry?" she screams. "Who's angry? I'm not angry!"

REACTION

On the day John F. Kennedy was shot down on the streets of Dallas, I was a young editor working in a newspaper office in Oklahoma City. The newsroom, after the chaotic rush to get out a special edition detailing the tragedy, was silent as a tomb. Across the room from me somewhere was Claire, a reporter who, I knew, had revered the fallen president.

Suddenly, I heard loud and inappropriate laughter racket across the room. Turning in shock, I saw that it had come from Claire. I was horrified.

It was only much later that I realized she had been in reaction without, of course, any awareness of what she was doing. In her extreme grief, she had suddenly started reacting against her painful feelings by *acting just the opposite.*

Why? Perhaps she simply could not fully face her pain. But the protection of simple denial failed her. The feelings broke through and were *there*, overwhelming in their intensity. And so she turned to her next line of psychological defense, a reaction which showed her acting out the precise opposite of what she was really feeling, almost as if by pretending to be happy, she might be.

Irrational? Of course. But there are parts of us that have little if anything to do with rationality or logic. We live with these parts of our personality, too. Sometimes when the pressure is too great, rationality breaks down and these more primitive modalities of survival break to the surface, ruling us.

Probably you can think of many cases in which you have witnessed, or even taken part in, such reaction: the uncontrollable urge to giggle during a solemn lecture or ritual; the burst of anger out of sadness, when you really feel defenseless and weak; a rush of bitter invective toward a lover when your heart is breaking and your basic emotion is anything but hateful.

In your novel, the shy, frightened young woman might suddenly begin flirting like Scarlett O'Hara, or the equally scared man might strut like a Don Juan. They—and the characters surrounding them—might be puzzled or shocked by their behavior. But *you* will understand the process driving them, and readers will recognize the truthfulness of your characterization on an instinctive level, even if they don't have the words to describe what they recognize.

DISPLACEMENT

Displacement behavior is one of the most interesting and useful patterns for the writer of fiction. Here—as in the other syndromes mentioned—the character is trying unconsciously to protect herself from facing feelings that simply are not acceptable to her. But in this case, the feeling or impulse is expressed—but in a disguised way or aimed in the wrong direction.

Examples? When my children were young, I often noticed that arguments broke out among them when I told them it was time to pick up their toys and go to bed. Invariably one accused another of making the toy mess, the one accused turned to blame his little sister, and all hell broke loose. But in actuality, assignment of guilt had nothing to do with the fight that took place. What really was happening was this: They didn't want to pick up the room. They didn't want to have to go to bed. They were angry at *me*. But attacking me was unacceptable behavior. So they displaced their anger and argument onto one another.

In one of my novels my hero, highly frustrated by the heroine, had a scene with her in the fenced back yard of a house. He argued and pleaded and she was sniffy, cold and thoroughly irritating. My hero got madder and madder and more and more frustrated until he was clearly about to explode. Finally, when she said something ultimately insulting, he balled his fists, trembled from head to foot, turned *and attacked the board fence.* This was a funny scene, but also true to life as he displaced his rage onto the only thing nearby which he could hit without being "a bad person."

Or consider another example. A young woman yearns for

family love and closeness, but is denied. She enters a religious order and becomes "a bride of Christ." This is not to suggest that all or even very many nuns enter the convent for reasons anything like this, but it's possible. In such a case, the impulse toward family and possible marriage and sexuality are for whatever reason not acceptable. So the impulse is directed into another sector—the religious life. Classic displacement.

You may frequently find occasions in your novels where the character would be too obvious or predictable if she showed exactly what was on her mind. A villainous character, especially, may need to make moves that are baffling and confusing to everyone, the reader included. You may wish to consider the psychology of that character in terms of displacement. Maybe he doesn't really mean to attack our hero at all; maybe he's mad at his wife and they don't own a kittycat for him to kick!

The psychology section of your favorite bookstore is sure to contain dozens of titles that include descriptions of other behaviors you might find equally interesting or useful, characteristics that are all, to some degree, neurotic behavior patterns. But they are as common as apple pie. Use them in good health. They'll help you complicate your major characters, and because they are so common, readers will see and understand them easily enough, without serious prejudice against the character so afflicted.

A note of warning, however: Some of the books you may encounter will go into clinical detail about behaviors much more serious than the ones I've mentioned. When you study these psychoses and try to put them into your stories, you're getting into very deep water indeed—and run a much greater risk of losing or alienating your readership.

A little craziness, in other words, is "normal" enough! Too much may be, well, too much.

TRANSACTIONAL ANALYSIS AND LIFE SCRIPTS
The theory behind Transactional Analysis can be very helpful to you in deepening your story characters.

Transactional Analysis, or TA, as it is often referred to, is so called because its founder, Dr. Eric Berne, observed in his psychiatric practice that clients related to one another in therapy groups in ways characteristic of their ways of relating in outside life. By analyzing group therapy transactions, Berne decided, he and group members could uncover—and analyze—the way people function with each other generally.

This led to Berne's development of games theory, the idea that people functioning unhealthily with others often played games—repetitive, self-defeating procedures that made real human contact impossible and "paid off" in bad feelings all around.

While game analysis is an invaluable therapeutic tool and very useful for the novelist who goes beyond the basics, the greatest value of Transactional Analysis is in the theory Berne developed as an underpinning for his observations. He theorized that our conscious minds are divided into three distinct "ego states," and how we feel and behave depends to a large degree on which ego state happens to be ascendant in us at any given time.

Berne called these ego states the Parent, the Adult and the Child.

These have little or nothing to do with classical Freudian psychology, which places so much emphasis on unrealized or unconscious feelings and motives. Berne says we can become conscious of the different voices or impulses within us if we analyze the way we interact with people and work hard to be more aware of our different kinds of feelings.

In TA theory, the *Parent* ego state is the seat of nurturing impulses, whether directed toward yourself or someone else. It may also express itself in critical comments of the kind that might be concluded with a statement such as, "I'm telling you this (or suggesting this) for your own good!"

The *Adult* ego state is a data processor, that part of our personality that's ascendant and in charge when we take in factual information and deal with it in an objective way. For example, when you ask someone what time it is and they tell you, it's an adult-to-adult transaction. The Adult also listens to internal dialogues between the Parent and the Child.

The *Child* ego state is the seat of emotion, creativity, willful impulses, manipulation—just about all those aspects of personality which make us appealing (or otherwise!), but which also can often get us in trouble. When we really play, we are said to be "in our Child." So, too, it is the Child who loves, hates, laughs, sings and envies.

The goal of healthy functioning, according to Berne and many who have followed him, is to be able to move from one ego state to another at will, depending on the situation and what ego state *cathexis* (energizing and putting in command) is appropriate. In a daylong business conference that begins with analysis of budget data, includes a lunch at which one provides loving sympathy for a worried employee, and concludes with a dance party, for example, it might be appropriate to be in the Adult ego state for the data session, the Parent for the lunch, and the Child (with the Adult hovering near for self-control) during the party.

Using the fundamentals of TA can give you another basis on which to found puzzling character behavior. Your female lead, for example, may show a lightning change from near-maternal concern to a foot-stamping outburst of childlike disappointment, given the right stimulus to trigger such a dizzying change. Or you might show the cold-hearted accountant (in his Adult ego state) become a nurturing parent to a sick child (in his Parent state), seemingly "changing spots" with amazing quickness that will ring true to the reader even while surprising her.

CROSSED TRANSACTIONS

Understanding of this basic TA theory also allows you, the writer, to search for additional sources of conflict in your story. You do so by trying to set up what analysis practitioners sometimes call a *crossed transaction*.

To illustrate: Earlier I mentioned a transaction that might go like this:

> HE: "Pardon me, dear, but what time is it?"
> SHE: "It's eight o'clock."
> HE: "Thank you."
> SHE: "You're welcome."

A harmonious exchange of information, a transaction of Adult-to-Adult.

But what if you want to inject a hint of conflict into it?

Knowing TA theory, you might do it like this:

> HE: "Pardon me, dear, but what time is it?"
> SHE: "Damn! I'm so mad at you!"
> HE: "What did I do? What—"
> SHE: "I'm sick of your asking me things! Don't you know I'm busy and tired? You don't care anything about me!"

Now an argument has started, perhaps, or at least there's an element of conflict, because the lines of the transaction have been crossed.

In the first example, he asked from his Adult and she replied from her Adult. This illustrates the principle of the *complementary* transaction: The ego state which is addressed is the one that replies, and such transactions often proceed quite harmoniously.

In the second example, the transaction is crossed up. He still asked out of his Adult. But she responded with anger out of her frustrated Child. Thus, the lines of communication crossed. And when the transaction is crossed like this, an argument is likely not only to start but to continue almost indefinitely, because the different ego states can't understand one another. Nothing ever gets accomplished.

Understanding this principle allows you to create conflict out of the simplest transaction between story people, with resulting confusion and bad feelings. And on another level of your awareness as a writer, it's always good to be aware of what ego state your people are in as they maneuver, worry and square off.

Let me hasten to add that they don't have to be in different ego states for conflict to occur. Two people, gravely concerned about a third, might differ radically about the best way to "parent" the third party with help or advice—or by leaving the third person alone. Or there can be serious disagreements about how to analyze company sales figures, for example—an Adult-Adult transaction. Both parties can be in their Child, one trying cleverly to manipulate, the other having a temper tantrum. But it's the crossed transaction that can provide you with some wonderful additional conflict when there may actually be very little basis for it in story reality.

THE DRAMA TRIANGLE

In setting up conflicts in your novel, another theory growing out of Transactional Analysis may help. That's the idea of the "Drama Triangle," as outlined by S. Karpman in the *Transactional Analysis Bulletin* in 1968. It's suggested that two or three people can get into all kinds of trouble with one another by assuming conflict roles. The roles are usually identified as the Persecutor, the Victim and the Rescuer.

Once you've set up a Drama Triangle for your characters, you can make all sorts of interesting and dramatic things happen.

Suppose, for example, Dad walks in to find son Billy making a mess in the kitchen while Mom is in the utility room. Dad yells at Billy. Billy starts to bawl. Dad is the Persecutor and Billy is the Victim. But now things get more complex because Dad suddenly changes positions in the Drama Triangle and starts explaining to Billy that he (Dad) is really just trying to "rescue" Mom from extra work. Puzzled by Dad's change of roles, Billy falls silent. In rushes Mom. She sees Billy's tears and launches into her Rescuer act, at the same time becoming Persecutor to Dad, saying something like, "What have you done to the poor child now?" Dad—now suddenly thrust into the Victim role—starts to sulk, retreats from his Parent ego state into his Child and slinks out of the room, muttering, "I was Only Trying to Help." (His favorite game.) At which point Mom sees the mess Billy was making and starts screaming at him (another game usually called "Now I've Got You You Son of a Bitch"), thus taking on her Persecutor role. Billy then yells that she should have stayed out of it (becoming her Persecutor, which makes her suddenly the victim playing another popular game, "Poor Me").

You can see how this sort of unhappy struggle can go on indefinitely. The only thing required is for all participants to be willing to change roles at the drop of a hat. Unfortunately, people do this all the time in real life—and that's good for you as a novelist, because that means you can have your story people do the same thing any time you feel the need to stir up more trouble in your plot.

As an exercise, take some time out and practice with one of your own characters, putting down a few things he might say or do when he is in each of his ego states.

Then take two of your characters, put them in the same imagined room, and experiment with having them suffer through crossed transactions and possibly even a fight based on the Drama Triangle.

These exercises sound simple and easy to skip. I hope you won't skip them. They can cement your understanding of these methods of making your story people more complex and interesting.

THE LIFE SCRIPT

Before we turn from TA theory, there is one more aspect of it that should be discussed. This one can be invaluable in building character background. It's the concept of Life Script.

According to Berne's theory, exquisitely amplified by Claude M. Steiner (in his book *Scripts People Live*) and others, people very early in their lives, and without realizing it, draw conclusions about reality and the people around them, and mentally write a script for the way their life is going to be.

Messages of two kinds come to the small child from parents and significant others. Some of these are positive moral precepts and advice, which flow from the Parent of the parents to the little one. These are called Drivers, and include such things as "Work Hard," "Be Perfect" and "Try, Try Again." These are usually given verbally, and grownups will often be heard repeating family Drivers as if they were gospel.

At the same time, however, negative feelings and attitudes may flow nonverbally from the Child of the parents to the little one. These are called Injunctions. The message may be lethal. Common ones include "Don't Grow Up," "Don't Feel," "Don't Be Important," "Don't Make It" and the most lethal of all, "Don't Be."

Sometimes, good-sounding Drivers automatically carry a near-lethal Injunction. The little one urged to try to "Be Perfect" obviously can never succeed; the task is impossible. So the person with a "Be Perfect" Driver will always carry along a "Don't Make It" Injunction as well.

Taking in the Drivers and Injunctions, making decisions on the basis of childhood intelligence, the person forms her life script, is seldom aware of its implications, and can go through life making crucial decisions just as if she really were carrying a printed script in her hands.

For the novelist, devising pictures of the character's early home life, the Drivers and Injunctions and the resulting character script, is an amazingly useful tool. What kind of a life script is your most important character carrying through life? Is it generally a healthy one? Is there some hidden injunction that might threaten her? How about your major antagonist, your villain? Did something in his life script contribute to making him the kind of person he is?

Therapists sometimes go so far as to draw up a chart from information supplied by a client. Such a chart includes names of parents, siblings, grandparents and others in the family history. It includes information about how those people lived their lives, what they did and what they failed to do, how they ended up. Sometimes such charts show a recurrent pattern of life script going back generations. You may wish to consider drawing up such a chart for the most important characters in your own novel.

FURTHER STUDY

A stroll through the Psychology or Human Development section of your local bookstore will turn up dozens if not hundreds of books on human personality. Some are good and some are awful. If you delve into such store sections, you'll be wise not to take seriously everything you read. On the other hand, you may find some facet of psychological theory that makes great sense to you, and then you can incorporate it into your work.

In addition, you might want to practice a bit more with the simple character devices suggested to you by this chapter. You might even create a couple of new characters demonstrating some of the complications mentioned here, and then put them together in a confrontation and see how they play off against one another.

If you do some of these things, it will be good for you. But as a final word, nothing is likely to be as helpful to you as a novelist as keen-eyed *observation*—observation of others and of yourself. Of all the things you put into your work journal as time goes by, your observations and thoughts about yourself and the people around you may become the most precious in terms of becoming story material.

I won't make it an assignment to go out right now and observe people—and to try to look honestly into yourself. I'll just fervently hope that you've already been doing it.

Dialogue and Narration

Y ou may have considered it odd, on scanning the table
of contents of this book, to see "Dialogue and Narration" listed as late as chapter fourteen. Some other
books about fiction technique discuss these subjects
quite early.

I've delayed detailed discussion of these seemingly fundamental matters for two reasons. First, the ability to write good
dialogue and narration today is not as simple as it once was;
and second, you really need to understand a lot about such
things as scene structure and characterization before you can
get the most out of any close look at dialogue and narration
techniques.

No need to get uptight, though. Armed with what you
already know, you can incorporate this new information into
your technical arsenal without undue pain. And dialogue and
narration follow the same general principles that you've
already begun to use in your work, so once you've learned
them you're well down the road to knowing about the others.

Let's consider dialogue first.

Most modern novels are filled with scenes, and most modern scenes contain a lot of dialogue. Novelists today show conflict in the dialogue. They also use dialogue more than any
other single device to advance the story and characterize the
story people.

(Note that dialogue is *not* used as a "fact crutch," in which
story people lecture each other about things the writer wants
the reader to know.)

DIALOGUE IN SCENE

So good dialogue is vital to most contemporary novels because it's the lifeblood of most contemporary scenes. Story people talk, argue, maneuver, reveal or hide their real motives and struggle through conflict couched largely in story conversation. Since conversation takes place within the structure of scene, we know it must be reported moment by moment, with no summary. Moment-by-moment action (including dialogue) should be written following the rules of stimulus and response. Stimulus-and-response transactions may include brief internalizations by the viewpoint character when the stimulus is complex. So—putting together things we already know and applying them to dialogue—we already know a lot about how to write it.

Dialogue can be defined as story people talking.

Assuming that most dialogue takes place in scenes—

- It should be written moment by moment, with no summary.
- It should follow the rules of stimulus and reponse.
- It may include internalizations by the viewpoint character.
- It should involve conflict between the speakers.

DIALOGUE OUTSIDE OF SCENE

You have to remember, however, that everything in your book is not a scene. You will also have sequels. In addition, you may have any number of incidents—brief events which don't have much, if any, impact on later developments in the story, but which have to be presented for some reason.

Dialogue can also take place in these other story components. For example, your heroine, just out of a disastrous scene in which she lost a big murder case, might encounter her friend Harry in the courthouse hallway; he might ask why she is so upset and she might explain, the two of them having a nonconflictful (nonscene) talk about what just took place. This might be a mere incident.

Or you might take this same hallway meeting and give it virtually every element of a scene—even to having Harry be antagonistic and creating conflict—yet the *function* of the meeting and dialogue would end up working as *sequel*, in which your heroine talks about her emotional reaction, her thought processes, her new planning and even her decision toward new action in the coming scene.

And sometimes dialogue might occur in segments simpler than either of these examples, a brief chance conversation about the weather between Brett and her landlord on the front steps of her apartment building, for example, put into the novel merely to show normal, humdrum events as backdrop for the other 99 percent of the story.

THE COMPONENTS OF DIALOGUE

Dialogue consists of four possible component parts:

1. The words that are spoken
2. Attribution—the "he said" or "she said"
3. Stage action—gestures, movements, facial expressions and the like
4. Internalization—the thoughts and feelings of the viewpoint character during stimulus-response transactions.

The words that are spoken are presumably the heart of any dialogue scene or incident. But as we noted in chapter four, the spoken words alone can get abstract or confusing very fast unless the reader is also kept abreast of who is involved, where they are, who is saying what and how it all looks to the viewpoint character. You may remember the comment back there to the effect that writers often forget to put on paper what they are seeing in their imagination, with the result that the reader gets lost even as to who is talking.

USE OF ATTRIBUTION

Thus, at the most basic level, you have to keep clear in the reader's mind who is saying what to whom. The simplest way to do that is with direct attribution, as—

> "What time is it?" Joe asked.
> "It's six o'clock," Mary replied.

And, having once established that it's Joe and Mary talking, you might get by with two or three more exchanges between them without attribution, such as—

"Then I'm already late to work."
"You have to be there at six?"
"I'm afraid so."

Go much further than an additional exchange or two, however, and your reader will begin to forget which person spoke when. Have you ever had that terrible experience even in a published novel? You follow the dialogue through two or three nonattributed exchanges, and then you think, "Wait, who's talking here?" So then you have to backtrack with your index finger, thinking something like, "Okay, she said that . . . so he must have said this . . . so she said *that*," until you've gotten things straight in your mind again.

Which establishes a truth about readers and dialogue: you have to keep them constantly reminded about who is saying what.

Well, you can do that by putting in direct attribution every three or four paragraphs, and some novelists do just that. It may be enough. The problem, however, lies in the need to keep the reader aware of more than mere speaker identity. The reader needs to get some tips about how things are going physically—how the speakers may be moving or looking or grimacing. And that's where stage action comes in.

STAGE ACTION
Stage action doesn't have to be very dramatic. It might be a statement as simple as "Mary frowned" or "Joe's lips quirked in a smile." It might show real movement, such as "Mary turned, crossed the big office to the windows and looked out at the falling snow." Or it might be a simpler physical action such as "Joe pointed his finger at her." In any case, it gives the reader a brief look at something happening onstage during the story talk as it moves along. And that helps the reader stay oriented—imagining the scene as it plays out.

The beauty of stage action, however, is that it can accomplish more than reader orientation. It can also be used as an *identifier* for spoken words, eliminating much direct attribution.

Suppose, for example, you have just written part of a dialogue transaction in which Joe and Mary talked, and you already have several "he saids" and "she saids" but don't feel quite safe throwing in much unattributed dialogue. You could use stage action as the identifier, changing our original Joe and Mary transaction to something like this:

> Joe suddenly looked worried. "What time is it?"
> Mary glanced at her watch. "It's six o'clock."

Here you haven't had to "use up" another direct attribution—which we all worry the reader might notice and consider clumsy if repeated too often—and at the same time you've given the reader the briefest look at the physical side of the scene under way, helping to reorient him. So you get double duty from stage action.

Usually, however, such stage action should be kept very brief. There's a danger that if you put in too much between spoken words, you will lose track of what the conversation is about. In addition, note that stage action usually *should precede the spoken words*.

Why? Because it will keep your transactions more straightforward if you set them up so that the receiver of the stimulus can respond to the last part of the stimulus package just sent to him. Unless you want your second character to respond to the stage action instead of the spoken words, it makes things clearer to put the words last.

INTERNALIZATION

As mentioned earlier, your viewpoint character is also going to be thinking and feeling during a dialogue transaction. Often it helps the reader's orientation to the scene if you show, now and then, what these thoughts and feelings are as the talk goes along. And as also mentioned, it works best when you show these brief internalizations in normal stimulus-response mechanism that is following a complex stimulus.

So, going back to Joe and Mary again, suppose Mary is the viewpoint character (She *has to be* as we wrote it the last time, because we showed Joe's facial expression!) If we want to add internalization showing why Mary might make a more complicated response, we might write it this way:

> Joe suddenly looked worried. "What time is it?"
> Mary realized he had forgotten his watch again. She was sick of his carelessness. She glanced at her watch.

"It's six o'clock, and I'm getting tired even of being in the same room with you!"

So the internalization not only further orients the reader to Mary's viewpoint, but explains why she responds in a huff.

Here, however, it's even more important to put the internalization ahead of any other dialogue transaction component. If you put the internalization last, the reader is likely to be confused because he expects the response to be to the last stimulus, and *the respondent can't possibly respond to something the viewpoint character was thinking or feeling.*

MIXING AND MATCHING THE COMPONENTS

This is so fundamental, yet so often not observed in practice, that it's worth stating the technique in a different way. You may have a transaction using any of the following components:

The spoken words alone
Both spoken words and attribution
Spoken words and stage action
Spoken words, attribution and stage action
Spoken words and internalization by viewpoint character
Spoken words, attribution, internalization and stage action
Spoken words, internalization and attribution
Spoken words, internalization and stage action

Whatever pattern you use, you should be aware that attribution may not be necessary if you use stage action or internalization, or both, because they can be used as speaker identifiers. This fact should be a comfort to new novelists who tend to worry a lot about having too many "she said" and "he said" on every page.

Which pattern will you use? It will depend on, among other things, the kind of dialogue you happen to be writing at the moment. Intense, conflictful dialogue will tend to drive the viewpoint character into more frequent brief internalizations as the pressure mounts. Such dialogue will also possibly result in one or both characters showing stage action such as changes of facial expression, gestures, movement around the room or even more violent physical responses. A quieter, informative conversation in the story, on the other hand, may require more direct attribution because emotions are cool, stimuli are not as complex and stage action, realistically, should be very calm and undemonstrative.

How you "mix and match" dialogue components will also depend on the kind of story you're telling and the kinds of people involved. In a love story, keeping the reader aware of the viewpoint character's feelings may be enormously important, and so you would write dialogue with many emotional internalizations. On the other hand, in a spy story you might be writing about characters who keep their emotions under stern control—and your plot might require that you not tell too much of what the viewpoint character is thinking, for fear of letting the cat out of the bag.

MAINTAINING CLARITY

But however you mix and match, remember the need for clarity. Here are three easy observations that might help you in that regard:

1. Put all parts of a dialogue component in the same paragraph. Whether you have just the spoken words or several other components, think of the entire package as a single *stimulus* unit. When you've finished showing what that character feels or does or thinks or says, end that paragraph and start a new one for the response from the other character. And when that character is finished, paragraph again.

2. Keep each component as brief as you can by limiting each response to a single aspect of the conversation. *Don't* allow a character to make a speech in which eight ideas are expressed; only confusion can result. Let him state one thing, and have the other character respond to that. Break it up a step at a time.

It sometimes helps to think of modern dialogue as a tennis match. If one player hits one ball across the net and the other returns it, the game can be played. If a player sends ten balls across the net at the same time, it's chaos.

3. Place the dialogue component to which you want a response last in the paragraph. I said this once, but it's a principle so basic yet so frequently violated that I feel the need to say it again. Stimulus and response simply can't work if you forget this.

BODY LANGUAGE

Your life experiences and newly sharpened abilities to observe real-life people will help greatly with providing good stage action in dialogue. If you feel the need for more help in this area, however, it's readily available.

A number of years ago, writer Julius Fast wrote *Body Language*, which might have also been called *Tips on Stage Action for New Novelists*. The book remains in print to this day because it offers many fascinating insights that many others also have found useful and informative. There might be a copy in your local library, although a borrowed copy can't be marked up and kept close at hand the way a paperback copy can. And now that you know a smattering of Transactional Analysis, you might also find a more detailed and scientific book of interest. David A. Steere's book, *Bodily Expressions in Psychotherapy*, goes deeply into all sorts of hints—and changes in posture and body alignment—that tip off otherwise hidden emotional reactions as well as the ego state a subject may be in. This book, complete with many sketches of subjects, is a gold mine for the novelist looking for rich detail in the area.

ADDITIONAL DIALOGUE DEVICES

Finally, here are a few additional ideas about good dialogue in general. They can be stated as suggestions.

To link elements of dialogue, you may wish to—

1. Use question and answer. When one character is questioning another and the second character is being at all responsive, the dialogue units link tightly.

2. Allow one character to interrupt the other. When Bart starts to say something and Karen breaks in, the link is tight and immediate, as in this example:

"As I was saying to my mother—"
"Do we always have to talk about her?"

3. Use repetition of key words. The characters in dialogue can pick up on key words from one another, and their repetition syntactically ties the exchanges together.

Example:

Karen said, "I want a divorce."

"A divorce?" Bart echoed. "I don't understand!"

"You never have understood."

"Never? I don't see—"

"Damn you! You never see!"

"All I can see is that I love you—"

"Love?" Her expression was bitter. "You don't know what the word means."

Because he depended so heavily on dialogue, Ernest Hemingway's stories remain classic examples of brief, tight dialogue. So do Dashiell Hammett's. And, for that matter, F. Scott Fitzgerald's. Along with your study of current novels, you may profit from studying these masters.

PRINCIPLES OF NARRATION

Obviously, when your story people are not talking to one another, they will almost always be doing something, going somewhere, physically maneuvering, accomplishing something or trying and failing, interacting.

If the action taking place is at all important, it won't do to put it into tight, condensed dramatic summary. It should be developed as close to moment to moment as you can manage. Which may mean lengthy narration.

This can be difficult. Long passages of straight narration tend to get a little abstract for the reader. Such passages lend themselves to long paragraphs—which means oceans of "gray print" on the page—and readers tend to get impatient with that. I don't know about you, but I've often caught myself speed-reading—or even skipping through—long chunks of narration, even if I sensed it was fairly important.

To avoid such pitfalls, your first aim should be to remember all the ideas about dialogue just presented. You *can* make narration appear taut and interactive by following the rules of stimulus and response. Insofar as possible (and it's almost always possible), you should maintain a single, unified, identifiable story-person viewpoint in every given passage of narration.

USE OF OTHER ELEMENTS

In addition, remember that long blocks of narration can be broken up with the insertion of *dialogue fragments*. For example, in a long narration of a cross-country trip in an automobile, there's no reason why you can't break it up by inserting brief passages such as the following:

(After perhaps a page or two of narration—)

> He was very tired when they reached Tulsa at three o'clock in the morning. He slowed for the turnpike tollgate and Jennifer awoke beside him.
>
> "Where are we?" she asked.
>
> "Halfway there."
>
> She yawned. "Are we on schedule?"
>
> He decided to lie: "Yes."
>
> Leaving the tollgate, he sped up again. She sighed and seemed to go back to sleep. He knew he had to stop for gas soon, but decided to get the city behind them. Seeing the speedometer reach the limit. . . .

It's quite possible, too, to use straight-narration sequences as a frame for *sequel thought* and *plot review*. Remember that the viewpoint character is not only reacting to whatever is happening at the moment. Unless the action is intense, she will also be thinking. About what? About her characteristic preoccupation—the story goal and problem, an earlier scene disaster, unanswered questions and future plans. So by staying solidly in viewpoint you can become imaginatively aware of what the character would be mulling over during the narration portion. You can break up the possible monotony of a long passage by inserting sequel. This will not only keep your character internally busy, it will provide you, the author, with a valuable opportunity to review and analyze and characterize.

Narration may also serve a purpose other than the telling of story movement or events. It can help establish story mood. The most obvious way to use narration as a mood-enhancing device is by insertion of *setting description*. While your viewpoint character is on a trip or taking a long walk, or while he is exploring a new locale, or while two characters are maneuvering at long distance prior to the next big scene, you may find an opportunity for the viewpoint character to look around and notice details about his setting that he would not have time to notice during an intense scene, or even if heavily preoccupied in a major sequel. So, since the viewpoint character can notice, you can describe what he is seeing. What you choose to describe, how you say he is seeing it, and thus how you describe it, can contribute to the general mood of the story at that point.

Finally, you can to some degree control story pace with your narration. If you wish to give the reader a sense of speed and hectic pace, you can write short sentences and short paragraphs, insert very brief and tense bits of dialogue, portray desperate sequel preoccupations and describe the passing scenery in quick, choppy bursts. Contrarily, if you want to slow things down, you can assume a slower style with longer sentences and paragraphs, and use other insertion elements in ways to imply calm and slowness of pace.

There is always a danger inherent in narration, that of the writer falling into the trap of preaching at the reader about what the story "means" or how worried the reader should be at this point, or how pretty or ugly the setting is. Maintenance of viewpoint should eliminate this danger, but I have seen good writers get so deep into narration that they even allow a viewpoint character to get preachy. Remember always: The function of narration is to move the story along, to describe movement. If you allow it to become static or preachy, the game is lost.

PITFALLS AND SOLUTIONS

No discussion of narration, however, would be complete without a further word of warning. The modern novel has less of this element than it had in the past. Narration does generally tend to be less reader-involving than straight scene or sequel. And so it is a weapon to be used with great caution.

If you detect a sense of uneasiness in creating a long passage of narration, ask yourself two questions:

1. Can this segment be left out of the novel entirely?
2. Can this segment be recast into one or more scenes?

If the answer to either of these questions is "yes," then you might be wise to reconsider your plans and do something else entirely. But if you're *sure* you should proceed with narration, then remember the principles outlined here.

WORK TO BE DONE

Practice dialogue transactions, using various elements in various orders. Analyze published copy to see how the pros handle it.

Write two or three page-long sections of narration. Then try rewriting them, inserting dialogue fragments or bits of sequel material.

Look at your own novel plan to judge the need for whatever narration elements you may have in it. Be critical and ask yourself if everything you have planned for narration is necessary for the *reader*—not just for your own edification.

Sit back and give some thought to dialogue and narration—how their principles fit into the general picture of how a story works. Ask yourself questions like the following:

1. Am I using the right amount of dialogue for the kind of story I'm trying to tell?
2. Am I maintaining viewpoint at all times?
3. Is my narration based on stimulus and response?
4. Have I maintained pace during narration segments?
5. Am I sure I haven't used dialogue as a "fact crutch"?
6. Have I used narration to preach at the reader?

These are not casual questions. Your answers should not be "off the top of the head" in thirty seconds, either. Your conclusions should go in your journal.

PART THREE

Fine Tuning for Sales

Chapter Fifteen

Backstory and Hidden Story

Although young novelists probably don't often think about it, you seldom plot just one major story when planning a novel. Almost always, you end up plotting three: the *present story*, which is the novel your reader one day will actually read; the *backstory*, which is the history of events that affect the novel, but took place before your page one; and the *hidden story*, which is the record of events that take place during the present time span of your story, but offstage—out of the awareness of your viewpoint character.

The plotting of the present story is given the most attention, of course, but unless you are aware of the other stories involved—that in the past and that offstage—you can end up with a shallow or meaningless mess.

Even the simplest novel involves some background that the writer knows took place before page one. Most novels have considerable background, or backstory. On its most fundamental level, backstory may be the personal history of the major players, the sketchiest idea of the history of the setting, or some combination of the two. But as you delve deeper into your major characters, inevitably you make up more backstory for them. And I think the best novels are the ones which arise out of amazingly complex and detailed backstories—old events, old problems, old lies or deceptions or secrets—which have a direct impact on character motivations in the present.

The wise writer, then, will give considerable thought to her novel's backstory. If she is moving along in the first draft of her book and realizes she doesn't *have* much backstory, I think she should stop and work to invent one. The work will enrich her characters, her plot and her own sense of creative excitement. When you let your imagination run wild on details of the past preceding your novel, you may be astounded to "discover" all sorts of old secrets and hidden motives that enrich your plot.

PLANNING BACKSTORY

Sometimes the need for a detailed backstory is obvious to you as you write. In a recent novel of mine, for example, I simply had to have a case of mistaken identity between a brother and sister in order for my desired present suspense plot to work. Trying to figure out how this brother and sister could be born only a couple of years apart, yet never know of the other's existence, took me back generations in their family. A novel taking place during a few weeks in the nineties required my construction of a family saga in the backstory dating back to 1928!

If your story is of the type that requires considerable detailed backstory plotting, or if you decide to create a more complex backstory just to enrich the story, you must do it carefully and well.

The first step ordinarily is to type out a list of major backstory dates and what you imagine took place on those dates— births, deaths, major changes, shocks and setbacks, triumphs.

From this list (which often changes and grows many times during the planning), you may identify one part of one year, or a few scattered months, in which very important things happened. These brief periods may require more detailed planning.

An easy way to do this more detailed work is to use calendar pages. There are a number of simple, inexpensive computer programs available that will let you select any year in modern times and print out any month on a regular-size sheet of paper, each day represented by a blank block large enough for you to jot a lot of notes in. If you don't have such a program, you can draw your months with a ruler.

Having gone this far—identifying a real year and preparing backstory calendar note pages—you can (and should) consult a yearbook or history to allow you to pencil in a few major historical events. Is this important? It can be.

Example: You are writing a novel that requires backstory

including December 7, 1941; in outlining your backstory, you decide that date is Wednesday, and you have your backstory couple going to the grocery.

What's wrong with that? Most of you already know: December 7, 1941, the day Japan attacked the United States at Pearl Harbor, starting American involvement in World War II, was a Sunday. A *very* large percentage of your readers—and most likely the editor with the power of life and death over your manuscript—will know the truth and spot your mistake.

Of course, you might argue, you can't look up *everything* that might be involved somehow in your backstory; after all, you might end up letting the reader know very little of all the backstory stuff you look up. This is true. But you can't afford a major gaffe. I'm not suggesting a major research project here—just enough to be on the safe side.

Having gotten this far on backstory planning, I usually go a bit further and look up things like popular songs of the time, if that's appropriate, a bit about the weather in the region at the time, if possible and applicable, and even something about world events that might have been happening far from my story locale. Depending on the kind of story you're planning, you might want to do those things too.

Now the fun begins. Use your imagination to investigate the pasts of all your major characters and perhaps their parents or grandparents before them. Check your dates and chronology. *Be careful.* I once had a manuscript go through typesetting and all the way to the final check by a copy editor before anyone noticed that I had erred in dating part of my backstory. "Did your hero really father his first son at age eleven?" the copy editor called to ask me one day. (God bless copy editors!)

Don't expect to sit down and make up a detailed backstory in a day. This can be hard work. You may end up revising dates a number of times as you ask yourself questions like, "How old did grandma have to be in order to get married?" or "If Shirley was born in 1956, does that make her too old for this novel—and, if so, do I need to go back and change the date of her birth, and therefore the birth and marriage dates of her parents?"

You can get too enamored of planning backstory and get stuck in this stage of planning, with the result that you don't get on with writing your book. This is rare, however. Most new novelists err in the opposite direction, by not giving enough thought to backstory. You get more than plot ideas or help from working on it; often you stumble onto imagined backstory complications that give your characters extraordinary new depth.

TEMPTATIONS OF BACKSTORY

There are two more temptations about backstory that you must also learn to resist. One is to dump all your backstory into the present story just because you have the information. The other is to depend too much on old history for present motivation, thus forgetting the inexorable rules of stimulus and response.

The novelist who falls too much in love with backstory, and feels she simply must get it all into the present story, usually ends up with lots of flashbacks in her novel.

Flashback, however, is a much-overrated device.

A true flashback represents an author gimmick or intervention in the normal flow of the present story. It's usually a part of a sequel in which we literally flash back to previous events in the backstory and play them in the story *now* on a moment-by-moment basis.

There are two things bad about flashback. First, it's so damned obvious as a literary device, and so artificial. (If it weren't, why would all new novelists notice it and seem to worry endlessly about how to get one more in *their* novel?) Second, when you stop to flash back, you *stop* the present story—which is always dangerous in terms of possibly losing plot momentum and intensity of reader interest.

Flashback should never be shoveled into the narrative for its own sake. You can write a dozen fine novels and never use a single one. You should always look askance at the impulse to use a flashback just because you can, or because you know all this old stuff and dearly want to heap it on the poor reader's back somehow.

(Note that flashback as we've defined it here is different from summary of old events. Some of that may be necessary to keep the reader informed.)

So plan your backstory well. But use it for what it is, background. And always remember the point that was made as early as chapter six: Background is not stimulus. You can't fully motivate a character to do something in the present story of 1998, say, by saying something funny happened to her mother in 1950.

HIDDEN STORY: THE UNSEEN ACTIVITY

Hidden story is often even more necessary than backstory in working out your present story plot. It can be fun, and at the same time maddening, to plan.

The basic point to remember is that all your story people are doing something at all times during your present story. But most of them are probably offstage at any given moment. To make their entrances and exits "time out" correctly—and to allow you to plan the surprises they may be plotting offstage for the major viewpoint character—you have to know what they're doing at all times, even though most of their activity will never show up in the present story except in terms of the results.

For example, in timing your plot by cause and effect, it's mandatory to figure out what your villain is doing while the hero is onstage without him. If you want the villain to burst onto the scene at 4:05 P.M. in Cleveland, you may have to plan (while he isn't showing at all in the hero's viewpoint) that he decided the day before at 7:00 P.M. to go to Cleveland (which may require you to plot an unplayed scene or scenes and sequels to lead him to this decision); that he bought a ticket at 10:00 A.M. today; that he went to the airport at noon (which is why, perhaps, someone else onstage got no answer from his telephone at that hour, enhancing the mystery and worrying about his whereabouts); that his plane was late; that he arrived in Cleveland at 2:30 P.M.; that he got a taxi at 3:00 P.M.; and that it was 4:05 P.M. before he could possibly arrive in the present story awareness of your viewpoint character.

In writing his Travis McGee novels, John D. MacDonald faced serious limitations of movement and timing because he restricted himself to single viewpoint, first-person narration. In some of the earlier novels in the series, the pace gets wild and hectic because Travis has to shuttle from Fort Lauderdale to Maine to the Bahamas to Mexico in order to be onstage at all the right places and at all the right times to meet the other major players and witness all the major events while investigating the plot puzzles.

In later books in the series, MacDonald had an inspiration in the form of a new character, a former professor named Meyer who lives near McGee on the slips at Fort Lauderdale. Now, Meyer is phlegmatic and philosophical while McGee is highly active and results-oriented, so Meyer is a fine contrast to McGee, both their characters benefit by their contrast and some of the Meyer-McGee conversations are fun to read. But the *real* value of Meyer is that he can go offstage and run all kinds of errands for McGee and come back later out of the hidden story and report things he has found, places he has been, people he has met—giving McGee (and MacDonald, of course) a convenient errand boy into the hidden story.

Characteristically, McGee tells Meyer a problem, and Meyer vanishes for a while. McGee is free to interview people locally, get into all sorts of trouble and probably meet a fascinating woman. Then Meyer can come back and give a report that goes something like this: "When you were meeting Sacha on Tuesday, I was in Chicago, where I met a man named Jones. He told me to find a man named Kline in Boston, so on Wednesday, while you were fixing the broken bilge pump on the *Busted Flush*, I went to Boston, where at three o'clock in the afternoon he warned me that...."

You might not need an errand boy like Meyer. If you're not in first person, you might sometimes get away with changing viewpoint in a scene or a chapter to show the reader what some other character is doing or planning outside the main viewpoint character's awareness. However you handle things, though, you must plot your hidden story with almost the same care you use for the present one. Otherwise, at the simplest level of difficulty, you might end up with present-story outrages like having a character return from the hidden story with reports of activities that couldn't possibly have happened to him in the hidden-story time implied by his reappearance.

To put this another way, you must plot the hidden story:

- to prevent timing errors in the present story;
- to keep track of offstage planning by nonviewpoint char-

acters whose subsequent actions will show up in the present story;

- to plan logical story motivation for offstage characters by imagining sequels they must be having, even though viewpoint limitation prevents you from ever getting into their heads;
- to set up events and thinking offstage which will provide logical but unanticipated shocks for the viewpoint character when hidden story "chickens come home to roost."

USE OF CHARTS OR CALENDARS

As with backstory, a list, chart or calendar may be invaluable to you in planning hidden story. Often, in a complicated book with many vital characters scheming and maneuvering offstage, I have resorted to the use of lined plot-planning pages divided by a vertical line down the middle. I then assign each horizontal line on the page to a given day, or sometimes to a given hour or (if the plot action is really intense) a given ten-minute block of time. Next I sketch in, on the left side of the page, the times and major events in the present story. I then go back and sketch in on the right side the major events and times in the hidden story. Then I redo these sheets to neaten them up, closely showing how present-story timing relates to hidden story—that while my hero was driving to work at 7 A.M., for example, *across on the other side of the sheet*, on the same horizontal line, in the hidden story, the villain was slipping into the hero's office and starting to search it.

Such simple visual arrangement of present-story and hidden-story events often can enrich your imagining of how everything is playing out.

There are few aspects of novel-writing as challenging, yet as much fun, as plotting backstory and hidden story. Much more could be said about the matter. But this is another of those areas where you're getting a learner's permit here. If you want to delve deeper, you will.

ANALYSIS

A potentially rich learning experience awaits you if you'll again dig out the colored pencils and mark up a current novel. Mark all the statements about backstory in RED. Mark all reports from the hidden story in GREEN. If you find a viewpoint change, mark direct references to time (reader orientation pointers) in BLUE. At the point of such changes of viewpoint to usher the reader into the hidden story, ask yourself why the author felt such a shift into the hidden story was necessary.

As you do this work, I think you'll develop increasing respect for the amount of hidden planning that goes into every successful novel.

Chapter Sixteen

Story Architecture

Each of us carries around inside us our own private concept of what a novel is *for us*. As we learn more technique, this concept grows and changes. What your ultimate vision of a novel will be, or how you will one day define the architecture of a long story, can't be predicted. In this chapter, however, I want to bring together a number of ideas about the novel "construct" as it seems to me.

In chapter nine we took a long look at the major components of novel structure, scene and sequel. Now, with other information under our belt, we can consider some additional aspects of those crucial elements as they affect the general architecture of your book.

PLOT DEMANDS AND MANIPULATION OF SCENE-SEQUEL

Depending on where you happen to be in your novel's plot and what you want to accomplish in terms of effects on the reader, you may present scenes and sequels out of the normal predictable order outlined in chapter nine. Novelists always *plan* their books in the prototypical sequence of scene-sequel-scene-sequel, but they don't always *play* them in the normal order. Many variations from classic sequence are possible.

In that regard, some general observations can be made:

1. Scene and sequel do not have to be "played" in chronological order even though they were undoubtedly planned that way.
2. Scene can interrupt sequel, and vice versa.
3. A scene or sequel may be skipped entirely.

4. Scene-sequel structure is the key to how (and when) you change viewpoint.
5. Understanding of scene structure is the key to writing copy that's "hard to put down."

Each of these points deserves some elaboration.

Scene and sequel do not *have to be* presented to the reader in strict chronological order, and they seldom are.

The beginning writer tends to tell his story in summary, the way we report an interesting event in conversation. Most of the time, we also tell such oral stories chronologically, in the time-order in which the events took place.

One of the first things a fiction writer has to learn, however, is that straight summary is not involving enough for readers. As we have seen, some events must be developed moment by moment and "put on stage," as it were, for dramatic impact on the reader's imagination.

This discovery of the need for dramatic presentation alternating with periods of introspection eventually leads the writer to some understanding of scene and sequel structure. And what a day that is, because suddenly everything begins to make sense in terms of how to put long stories together!

At this stage in the writer's development, however, she often tends to present her scenes and sequels just as she first imagined and collated them—Monday, Tuesday, Wednesday . . . 9 A.M., 1 P.M., 6 P.M., etc. And this can be deadly because actually presenting the story in straight chronology often leads to a story that plods, gets predictable, is too even in tone and boring, and doesn't have the surprises and dramatic peaks that it should have. Even worse, there's a serious danger that the reader may figure out how she is being tricked into breathless suspense and gut-wrenching emotion through the structure. We can't have that. So while you plan your story from day one to the last action on the last day, you don't often present it that simply.

It may be, for example, that your novel outline shows hero Andy meeting his lover (scene 1); realizing he is in love with her and agonizing over what he is to do about his marriage (sequel 1); trying to call her later and finding she has gone somewhere (scene 2); worrying about his weakness and perfidy as he heads home (sequel 2); trying to patch things up with his wife and instead being tossed out (scene 3); feeling bad as he moves out (sequel 3); meeting his lover to cheer himself up but learning that her plans definitely do *not* include living with him on a committed basis (scene 4); feeling really horrible (sequel 4); *while you as the author know* that in the hidden story, at the same time Andy is seeing his lover and learning the horrible truth, his wife is talking to her lawyer about what she should do next (scene 5); has thought about it (sequel 5); and has now gone to the bank to withdraw all the funds in the couple's joint account (scene 6).

Even this simple sequence of events can't be played chronologically, however, because if you do so, there are at least two things wrong: (1) the story gets predictable fast, and (2) you're in trouble when you try to be chronological with events that your planning charts show are happening at the same time.

What to do? Obviously, "play" the scenes and sequels for better dramatic effect and/or clarity and/or mystery.

Possibly you open with Andy's viewpoint as he confronts his wife, and the reader is immediately plunged into a harrowing scene between them. (Notice, you have skipped several things already.) Perhaps then you skip time (and viewpoint) to show Andy's wife seeing her lawyer, you skip the sequel to that for the sake of speed and send her off "somewhere," but you hook the reader by not telling him where. Then perhaps you show Andy learning the bitter truth from the lover, and in his sequel to that, you have him review his earlier dreams— and *play for the reader at this late stage a dramatic summary or even a flashback scene* showing his earlier meeting with the woman in which he realized he loved her. Then, perhaps, you have him finish a later sequel, insert a bit of dramatic summary or narration, and the next thing the reader knows, it's two days later and you can leap straight to another scene between Andy and his wife, or him and his lawyer.

So what you *planned* might be straightforward, but for various dramatic reasons, what you present to the reader might be far different. The result of all such mis-arrangement of scene and sequel is that the reader gets the big moments in the order in which maximum impact will be derived and at the same time is kept constantly off-balance. Another example, this from a published work, may clarify things further.

In her novel *The Trembling Hills*, Phyllis A. Whitney takes us to the brink of a scene in which the young heroine is about to walk into a room and confront an aged and formidable matriarch with information about their blood kinship. The narrator is scared about the impending scene, and we as readers are on edge. She walks into the room to face the old woman—and the chapter ends.

We turn the page, breathless to see the scene unfold—and find ourselves at a family dinner many hours later, with the principals talking about something else altogether!

We read well into this *considerably later* scene before the narrator says, in effect, "It had been harrowing, facing my grandmother, but when I had walked into the room that afternoon I had said. . . ." This puts the narrator:

- in a small sequel to something that had just played onstage during the evening dinner;
- reviewing during this sequel the scene that had taken place earlier in the day;
- playing that scene inside this later sequel for us now;
- and then going on—still in the mid-dinner sequel—to play for us the earlier sequel she had had after the earlier scene!

Phyllis Whitney has been one of our cleverest writers for decades, and the technique worked wonderfully—puzzling us, compelling us to read further, explaining when necessary, complexifying and deepening a sequence of events that might have been far less fascinating if told chronologically.

A note of warning about the use of this technique, however. You must never delay a big scene like this unless you are very clear in your mind that drama will be increased by playing it out of normal order. I say this because writers sometimes inadvertently skip or delay big scenes because they are hard to write—and for no other reason. So if you use this device, use it with good reason, and not to make things easier on yourself as writer.

If you think about this, study your own work, and analyze published novels, you'll quickly see that scene and sequel are always there, but—if the story is effective—often are almost invisible to the reader because they are not played one after the other, like link sausages.

INTERRUPTION OF SCENE OR SEQUEL

Scene can interrupt sequel, and vice versa.

As an example, in a novel I did many years ago called *Katie, Kelly and Heck*, there was a point in the book early on where I needed to motivate an essentially cautious and intelligent heroine to get mildly involved with a man who was obviously, in the language of the story era, a "bounder and a cad." How to do this?

First I set up a simmering animosity between Katie and another man in the story, Mike Kelly. Then I introduced my humorously oily villain, the other man, Ray Root, in a scene in which he asked Katie to go out with him. During this scene, Mike Kelly rushed in and tried to resume an earlier argument with Katie—to have *his* scene with her. So Mike's brief scene interrupted the Root scene. As a later result, Katie—to end her scene with Mike and spite him just as viciously as she could—recklessly turned back to Ray Root and accepted his oily invitation to go out.

So the Mike scene functioned as motive for Katie to do something stupid in the other scene, which it interrupted. *Scenus interruptus*, or something.

As for a possible *sequelus interruptus*, you have already seen earlier in this chapter how a sequel's normal pattern of development might be altered by the injection of a full-scale flashback scene.

You'll find many other examples once you start looking for them.

SKIPPING A SCENE OR SEQUEL

Pacing requirements may lead you to skip a planned scene or sequel. Three scenes may come one after the other so rapidly that the viewpoint character simply has no time for a developed sequel between them. Or for surprise you may skip a scene entirely to get on to an even bigger one.

You may *plan* it scene 1—sequel 1—scene 2—sequel 2—scene 3—sequel 3, for example, but you may actually present it as something like scene 1—scene 2—sequel 2—sequel 3, or in any other skipped order that enhances the dramatic effect.

But—let me emphasize the point—you still will have had to plan them all in order to have the material which you can skip or meddle with for greater effect.

Action-adventure stories often skip many sequels. Deeply psychological novels and many "literary" books often skip many scenes. That doesn't mean they're not all "there" in the planning. They're simply not all played, depending on the writer's intentions and the effects she wishes to produce.

TIPS ON CHANGING VIEWPOINT

Although today's novels increasingly violate the ordinary rules of maintaining viewpoint integrity within a scene, most writers, if they change viewpoint, still do so at some obvious break in the scene-sequel structure. Understanding scene-sequel structure is the key to how (and when) you change viewpoint, if you choose to do so.

Within either component, you will have a far easier time of it (and so will your reader) if you maintain the same viewpoint until the end of that structural component.

If you decide to change viewpoint at, say, the moment of scene-closing disaster, you can go to other viewpoints and insert a transition of many days or even months—and move the action halfway across the globe—and still bring the reader back to the original viewpoint clearly and without pain if you maintain structural integrity and *pick the character up again where you left him structurally*.

This is what I mean: Suppose you have a scene in which Reggie insists that the bank examiner reveal who stole the funds. At the end, the examiner says, "Okay, Reggie, I wanted to spare you this, but the thief is your missing brother."

Wham! Nice disaster. Nice place to change viewpoint. So let's imagine that you do so, going perhaps to the missing brother, to the hero's wife, to the bank examiner or perhaps to some other major character for some reason. In the time scheme of this other viewpoint, a week of story time passes. You as the author know that the hero, while offstage in the hidden story, has gone from Oklahoma City to London, England.

Big transition. Can the reader handle it? Sure. If you maintain structural integrity. Think: Where did we leave Reggie? At the disaster. So where must we pick him up, to keep things straight in the reader's mind? At the start of his sequel to that disaster, of course. So we come back to Reggie with a statement like:

Reggie was still reeling from shock and humiliation a week later as his British taxi stopped in front of London's Cumberland Hotel.

And the reader has no problem whatsoever with the transition across time and space because—in terms of structure—*nothing has happened to Reggie*: He is exactly where he would have been if his viewpoint line had been followed up immediately after the disaster.

Many readers don't understand scene and sequel. But oh, do they have a sense of it. And that sense—their almost intuitive grasp of story structure—makes changes of point of view and gaping transitions not only possible but easy as pie.

That's why scene and sequel structure are the key to writing copy that's hard to put down. You just leave a viewpoint at a disaster, go to another character and put her in a disaster moment; switch back to the first and get his reaction to his first disaster and show him walking into a likely new disaster; then switch back to the other character and take her to the point of decision and then leave her viewpoint again with a line such as "Then she knew what she had to do" and change viewpoint again, leaving the reader hanging as to what the character's new decision is—and you've got copy that keeps the reader turning the pages like crazy, being tricked again and again into suspense and worry.

VIEWPOINT-CHANGE TACTICS RELATING TO STRUCTURE

The best place to change viewpoint, in terms of building reader suspense, is immediately after the disaster.

Second-best probably is at the moment of new decision in the sequel, whether or not you choose to hold out on the reader as to what that decision is.

Third-best probably is during the decision-making process, when the character struggles with quandary.

A case could be made, in some books, for the best spot of

all being midway in the emotional hell of the sequel—if you're writing a book where the sequel really is hell and where you get deep into the character's emotions.

GENERAL PLANNING CONSIDERATIONS

Much of this chapter has presupposed something we discussed much earlier; that is, we all carry around a largely unexamined model of what a novel is for us. Part of our lifelong quest for excellence as writers should be examination of contemporary writers we admire, analysis of their techniques, and struggle to learn from them in order to grow clearer in our conceptualization and surer in our carrying-out of our own view of a novel.

I have noticed that a great many novelists seem to follow most of the following general assumptions about the ideal architecture for a novel. They prove in their work the following "rules":

1. *First, establish a person in a setting with a problem.* The person must be exaggerated, traited, tagged, with a background sufficient to drive her . . . and be bothered greatly by some change in her universe which has upset her equilibrium, threatened her self-concept and stirred her to fight.

2. *Make sure a threat is clear and pressing.* Here vagueness never helps, and if the threat can be put into the form of another character who is sinister or powerful (or both!), so much the better.

3. *Make the stakes high.* Little stories about little people with petty problems seldom sell today.

4. *Put the central character onstage, already in motion toward some specific shorter-term goal.* The shorter-term goal relates to the long-term goal, which provides the umbrella story question the reader will worry about throughout the novel.

5. *Keep the adversary or opponent active.* It's not enough to show him once; he must have a game plan and be rushing along to try to carry it out at the expense of the hero.

6. *Develop a sequence of scenes to bring in other characters and tighten the suspense.* Others enter because they too have much to win or lose; they take sides. The picture becomes muddier.

7. *Establish one or more subplots relating to the main plot.* People these. Work on the background of these characters and their

relationship to the hero and/or villain.

8. *Devise strong disasters to end scenes.* Good disasters propel the viewpoint character into sequels, and deepen the suspense. (Of course such setbacks also "hook" the reader.)

9. *Alternate viewpoints in the body of the novel.* But make sure that the primary viewpoint clearly dominates. There should be more scenes involving your main character than any other, for example. And sometimes, when you're in other viewpoints, those people should be characteristically preoccupied with the fate of the major player.

10. *Make sure the hero can't resign from the action.* Tighten the plot ropes around him. Increase his desperation. Show in sequel thinking that he *must* fight on because the outcome is essential to his self-concept and ultimate happiness.

11. *Set a ticking clock if at all possible.* If you can make the reader aware that time is limited or is running out, it adds to suspense. Perhaps it's as simple as one character saying to another, "I can't handle much more of this. I'm going to force a showdown Saturday night—twenty-four hours from now." Or it might be more sinister—a final ultimatum from rebellious convicts holding hostages, or the deadline for payment of a ransom. (In your reading, notice how often clocks are set.)

12. *Conclude with a decision in action.* As often as possible, follow Foster-Harris's concept of sacrificial decision, described in chapter eight. This will provide a smashing climax, out of which will come payoff excitement—and revelation of theme.

Your own emerging vision of the ideal novel may be different from the one implied in these few observations. If it is, can you write it out in terms descriptive of how you approach your material to get *your* effects? If you can't do a very complete job of this yet, it's something you should be starting on anyway.

DESCRIBING WHAT A NOVEL'S STRUCTURE IS FOR YOU

Try it now. Write down a description of what you think "your" novel is like. Sketch in an outline for it.

The outline may be vague and, in some places, may say things like "Here she usually falls in love." Fine! Test to see how clear you really are about your own vision. Believe me, the exercise may pay dividends for you in ways you can at this moment scarcely imagine.

Then, having gone this far, create your own list of a dozen precepts about the novel similar to the ones just above. Compare. Contrast. Think about it. Log your conclusions in your work journal.

But, as you work on your novel, remember that your vision may change. Trust your feelings. Don't discount sound professional advice, but don't change things at random, to please everyone in your class or at the local writer's club, either.

For ultimately it's your book, your baby. And that of your main character, too.

LETTING YOUR CHARACTER DO THE TALKING

Finally, you should realize that this kind of structural thinking and working can be very draining on you both intellectually and emotionally. It's possible to get yourself badly tangled up in thoughts and plans that get too abstract and confusing.

If that happens, you might try this: Draw up two chairs facing one another. Sit in one. Imagine your main character sitting in the empty chair facing you. Ask him or her—out loud—how things seem to be going.

Cross the room physically, sit in the character's chair, stare back at yourself, imagined in the chair you just vacated, and reply, again actually speaking the words aloud.

Cross the room again, letting the physical movement back and forth contribute to the hypnotic role-playing. Continue the dialogue.

You may feel foolish doing this, but all I can say is, it works. I have seen "stuck" novelists suddenly begin to feel that they are really talking to their character—and making all kinds of exciting discoveries about motivation and plot that they might never have made by coldly drawing charts and writing scene outlines.

If role-playing works for you—and it almost certainly will if you give it a fair chance—you can plan later how to fit your insights into your novel's more formal architecture.

WORK TO BE DONE

By this point you already know the kind of additional work I would prescribe—things like marking up another book and practicing more work such as scene interruption. By this time you also know I would be urging you to add observations to your work journal.

You're becoming a pro if you just go ahead and do the necessary work without having it spelled out for you.

Chapter Seventeen

Revision Techniques

There are as many ways to revise a novel as there are writers out there. There is no "standard" method, no "magic" method and no easy one, either.

Most of us stop and go back and fix something *only* if we've made a very, very major change in our plans, or simply can't go on until we work out some new plot or character assumptions on paper so we can figure out what's next. And we don't do this unless we *really* have to. Which results in a lot of truly messy first drafts out there.

Why do we insist on pressing on through the first draft at white heat? Because we know that good novels are not written but rewritten. We also know we'll discover necessary changes in the first draft that we couldn't possibly have anticipated. We know our conceptualizations of the characters will grow during the first draft, requiring that we go back to repair earlier, thinner character presentations anyway. We know that our first job is to put typed pages in the copy box so that we'll have something concrete to look at, shuffle, think about, pencil on, and finally recast and reprint.

So the first rule of revision must be: Write your first draft, *then* start worrying about revision.

FIRST FIXES

Of course, by the time you put that last page of the draft into the box, you will probably have all sorts of notes to yourself about things you know you have to fix: timing problems, changes in character perception, new assumptions you may have been forced to make about the backstory, major problems in pacing that you've sensed and perhaps other problems as well.

The first thing to do, ordinarily, is to go back into the manuscript and pencil in—or roughly type in as inserts—all these known "fixes." This will probably make your manuscript messier than ever, but don't worry about it.

ANALYTICAL FIXES

The next step (or group of steps) is more systematic. You need to go back through the manuscript—*preferably with printout pages because you see more on the page than you do on the screen*—and look for problems with at least the following list:

1. *Timing.* Make sure you don't have things happening at impossible time intervals, like a character reporting that he made a trip (in the hidden story) from New York to Los Angeles in four minutes. If you say somewhere that it took days for a character to make a sequel decision, make sure you showed days of plot time passing for *everyone* in the story.

2. *Logic.* Reexamine characters' motives for all their major actions as explained in sequels. Make sure they aren't deciding to do things for crazy reasons, for no reason or just for the convenience of you, the author.

3. *Characterization.* Examine major characters in terms outlined in this book. Do they have good tags? Are they introduced in the most vivid way possible? Are they exaggerated?

4. *Conflict.* Have you heightened conflict wherever possible, to avoid lapsing into dull, plodding narration without much point?

5. *High stakes.* Is your plot built on the highest possible stakes? Is there anything you can do to heighten them?

6. *Reader orientation.* Are you sure you've opened all your scenes by showing the reader where and when the scene starts, and who's onstage, so he's oriented? Have you shown vivid glimpses of the setting, big or small? Is any research needed?

7. *Pacing.* Does the suspense tighten? Desperation increase? Is a clock ticking near the end?

This is the briefest possible list. You should take plenty of time to build your own checklist. You know your work and its problems better than anyone. After making up your own expanded list, you should follow it, even if it means going back through the manuscript ten times, looking for one problem on each separate pass-through.

However long it may take you to work from your own expanded revision checklist, I think it's still a good idea to interleaf or otherwise insert your required changes if you possibly can. Even if you find a huge chunk of the story that strikes you as virtually "impossible," it's better at this point to make copious notes or inserts rather than to sit down and write a new "first-draft" chapter. Of course sometimes the changes are so drastic that you can't do anything but start over on a piece of the story. But unless your situation is really that bad, note-making and insertion is preferable to writing new "cold copy." You should be functioning almost as an objective *editor* through all of this, and when you sit down and start writing big new sections, you lose your editor's vision and become a confused writer again.

If you find that a subplot needs drastic cutting, "X" through pages.

If considerations of characterization or timing or logic require that you *must* create some entirely new pages, then of course you have no alternative but to write them. Even here, however, you should simply insert them in the manuscript where they belong.

THE COOLING-OFF PERIOD

At this point, days or weeks (or months!) after you began analyzing your first draft for flaws, you will reach a point where you can't think of anything more that vitally needs fixing. The impulse here is to start back through your manuscript, chapter by chapter, retyping everything neatly, in "final form."

Resist the temptation.

Take at least a week off from the project. Read a new novel or two. Do some research on that other story idea that's been percolating. Go to a movie, take a hike, play golf or stay in bed all day and be lazy. Do anything but consciously think about the manuscript now nearing completion.

You need this time to distance yourself from it so you can return to it with a clearer eye. Your unconscious mind also needs the time to relax and freewheel and work on remaining creative problems outside your consciousness, in its own mysterious way.

When you've forced this relatively brief period of vacation and begin to get really antsy and eager to get back to work, feel free to do so. But *do not*, please, rush back at that pile of pages with a red pencil or notebook.

READING LIKE A STRANGER

You've been away from it. Your view of the manuscript is going to be clearer. Now what you want to do is get a reading from that cooler, more detached perspective.

No one can ever see her work entirely as a fresh reader—a stranger—might see it. But this is your best chance. Try to read it as someone else would.

Here's how. Take the pages to your favorite reading spot. Make yourself comfortable, just as you did last week when you curled up with that new romance or thriller. If you usually sip tea while reading, get the tea. Try to duplicate your usual "fun reading" environment or approach it as closely as possible.

Then start reading your own pages. Have a small cassette recorder handy for notes, if you think you might need it. Don't use a pencil or a notebook. You didn't have those for your favorite author last week, remember.

Simply read. If you hang up, dictate a note into the recorder. If you have an idea for a fix, *briefly* dictate it, but don't get slowed down too much. You're a reader now, remember?

If you do this well, you may be able to read as many as fifty pages before you begin to tire and get too self-critical. When you reach that point, quit for the day. Resume tomorrow, same routine.

By the time you finish this reading, you will have found parts of the book you love, and perhaps some that you hate. But your sense of the flow and feel of the entire manuscript will be sharper than it has ever been.

FINAL NOTE-MAKING

Now, using your tape-recorded notes, do whatever additions, changes or deletions you thought were necessary during your reading. Insert these notes into your rough-draft stack of pages, just like all the others.

FINAL REWRITE

Having done all this, you are finally ready to start back through the manuscript, making the revisions on the keyboard, incorporating everything into a new draft. Work slowly, realize that you're probably tired by this time, and fight discouragement. You're almost home.

FINAL *FINAL* REWRITE

When you have a clean manuscript printed out, give yourself another few days off and try reading it again in your easy chair. You may find still another few things to fiddle with. If you do, fiddle away. At this point, almost surely, you can make any further changes by recasting only a page, a few pages or possibly one scene. The backbreaking work is behind you.

This kind of twiddling with the fine points can go on for a week or two, or somewhat longer. But clearly you know you are very near the point where you can let the manuscript go, content that it's as good as you know how to make it.

But when do you know for certain that revision is finally *really* all done? Writers often ask me that. I usually tell them to revise and reconsider increasingly smaller and smaller concerns and problems until they are so sick of the whole thing that they simply can't possibly go through the damned manuscript again. When you reach that point, you've probably finished your final, final rewrite.

OTHER OPINIONS

Now you face perhaps one more question that might affect the revision process. Do you mail the manuscript off, trying to sell it, or do you perhaps get a second or third outside opinion?

This is a matter for you to decide. Some very successful novelists today have just a few friends to whom they submit their manuscript when it is considered "finished." These friends read and offer criticism if they have any. The writer is free to take any suggestions or reject them.

Those who use such a "reader system" tell me they sometimes get fresh insights into something wrong that's still lurking in the manuscript, or perhaps a positive idea for making something good a bit better. But I've had other writers tell me that they couldn't possibly derive any benefit from friendly readers.

Two things I know: First, if you try using friendly readers, make it clear to them that you're not looking for praise, but reality. It doesn't help if they read your book only to tell you how wonderful you are. Conversely, make it clear that you're not asking them to play author themselves, or come up with criticism just for the sake of appearing productive.

Second, unless your local writer's club or group is *very* unusual, don't bother taking it there. After more than four decades in the business, I know of very few writer's groups that actually provide anything resembling useful, professional manuscript criticism.

AGENTS AND EDITORS

There are literary agents out there who advertise that they will read your new manuscript and offer advice and criticism for a fee. A few of these appear to be legitimate. Most of them are in the business of collecting reading fees, have never helped anyone sell a manuscript, and wouldn't know a plot premise from a rutabaga. So if you decide to try such an agency, for heaven's sake learn the names of several previous paying clients and talk to them. You might save yourself several hundreds of dollars and avoid a bushel of bad advice.

Editors used to be a gold mine of advice and professional criticism for new novelists. Unfortunately, today's publishing houses are so understaffed that editors seldom have the time to mess with a manuscript that appears to be unpublishable in its present form. Don't expect help from such sources.

On the other hand, if you get a letter of suggestions from a *reputable* publishing house, by all means consider the suggestions and criticisms very, very carefully. The fact that the editor took the time to write to you means that your manuscript was a near miss. If you can fix it as suggested, the same editor might take another look—and even buy.

Think about any criticism you do happen to get from any source, but don't let yourself be crushed by it. *Save all such communications*, preferably by leafing them into your work journal. If nothing else, over a period of time you may collect a number of such criticisms; if you look back over them and see that they're all saying essentially the same thing, then I would take their collective words very seriously indeed.

WORK TO DO

It's not too early to be working on your own revision checklist. If you've been doing all the assignments listed in this book, you already have in your journal a sort of guide sheet to the checklist. Go back through your journal. Start on the checklist if you haven't already done so. Plan to add to it as time goes along and you will continue to learn.

Chapter Eighteen

Getting It Sold

Everything in this book has been aimed at making you a professional writer—which means a writer who *sells* what he writes. If you failed to read the preface to this edition, you may have wondered why you did not encounter more chapters specifically addressing the question of how to place your manuscript after its completion.

As I said then, your first job is to learn to write a really good novel. Once you've done that, everything else gets easier. *Until* you've done that, everything else is impossible.

So we've been about first things first: learning how to *produce a product that will sell.* Sales methods and tactics are a different ballgame.

Your first job is to become a fully functioning professional writer, smoothly handling all the basic techniques. Once you've reached that stage in your development, you will not only be producing marketable copy; in addition, you'll be analyzing other writers' successes, learning even more from them, and honing your personal perception of what a novel is *for you.*

Inevitably, as you take these further steps, you'll have a clearer idea of the kind of book you can write well, with an excellent chance of selling it. And then you'll write your own best novel with a pretty clear idea of what kind of market you hope to hit with it.

Most new novelists proceed during this phase of their career by breaking in with a genre novel—perhaps a western, a romance, a mystery, a thriller, or a science fiction novel. It's far easier today to find a buyer for a recognized genre book than for a generalized "mainstream" story that fits no specific category in the publisher's list of upcoming books.

In your growing wisdom about your own writing and the successful books you admire, you will probably elect to produce a genre novel too. Once you've published one or two of these, you'll have additional experience and expertise, and you will then have the option of attempting to "cross over" into another genre or into mainstream, working with an editor already familiar with your work. This is the most common pattern for successful novelists. Best-selling author Jack Higgins, for example, wrote several rather thin thrillers as he learned his craft before breaking out with his classic *The Eagle Has Landed*, still a thriller of sorts but with a vastly bigger and more complex scope in terms of stakes, backstory and hidden story. Ken Follet, author of many big sellers, followed a similar pattern, writing a number of straight genre books as he grew and learned.

You can do the same.

YOU CAN SELL IT ON YOUR OWN

A primary guide for you as you begin to seek a market for your first novel is likely to be a standard market reference. On a regular basis, a subscription to a magazine such as *Writer's Digest* is a good investment. You may wish to visit your local library sometimes and browse recent issues of national publications like the *New York Times Book Review* to remain aware of what's selling and what kinds of books are being heavily promoted in the advertisements. Also, I've seldom met a successful writer who didn't have a copy of *Writer's Market* on his shelf. This publication from Writer's Digest Books actually comes in several varieties, each emphasizing a different sub-section of the sprawling publishing business. These books not only tell you who the publishers are and what they say they want; in addition, you can find the name of the editor most likely to be interested in your product. Armed with this kind of information, you can start trying to sell your novel on your own.

Conventional wisdom, of course, says you will need an agent. Unquestionably, having one helps. For that reason, some new writers start their sales effort with letters directed not to a publisher, but to one or more agents.

The usual method of contacting a prospective agent is to write a good, brief, "punchy" letter which says who you are, what your novel is about, and states that you're looking for an agent. Such a letter then asks the agent if she will look at a detailed synopsis, an outline and sample chapter, or some other sample of your work to see if she might consider representing you.

This has worked for a number of my former students. Most sent letters to ten or twenty agents, all at the same time. Out of one recent class, the student who had the best idea for a novel and the most intriguing letter (in my opinion) received five positive responses to the nineteen query letters he sent out. When he sent several chapters to one of the respondents, the agent accepted him as a client and promptly sold the book.

Agents are facing hard times these days, however, with the shrinking markets for some categories of novels. They tend to take on new clients less readily than they did in the past. So for my students who failed to find an agent after searching for one, I suggested sending the same kind of query letters to a broad spectrum of publishers.

This has worked for some of them, too. One, a man in his seventies, very recently placed his latest novel with a publisher after sending out more than twenty query letters and following up with sample chapters to the five or six publishers who said they would look at his work. One of my most successful students in the past, now author of several best-sellers, broke in by sending manuscripts to editors named in an edition of *Writer's Market*. Another woman reported her first sale not long ago after she had been sending her work out on her own *for more than ten years*. Her persistence paid off and she is now at work on a series under contract.

So possibly you can find an agent, but even if you can't just yet, selling your work on your own is not entirely out of the realm of possibility.

USE OF CONFERENCES FOR CONTACTS

Another of my former students just sold her second novel. Her first sale came after she made contact with a New York editor at a writer's conference in Oklahoma. He was there to give a lecture and look for talent. She met with him and told him about her work, and he allowed her to send it to him back in New York. He bought that first novel less than six weeks later.

Attending one of my favorite conferences, the one sponsored annually in Denver by the Rocky Mountain Fiction Writers, I've met several published novelists who got their start by attending that conference, meeting an editor and sending in work as a result of the meeting. When I was starting out, I secured the services of my first agent—who later made my first sales for me—as a result of our contact at a writer's conference. So I tend to be sold on them.

By all means go to a writer's conference in your area. Attend the sessions and learn. Talk to the editors and agents. Don't make a pest of yourself, but if you think you have a novel any of them might be interested in, let them know about it and ask if you might send them a sample chapter or two.

Talk to other registrants just like yourself, too. Ask them what other conferences they attend and how they rate them. Make notes. Send off for brochures. Evaluate them. Try another conference somewhere else.

You will quickly learn that some conferences are great and some are pretty awful. Consider this part of your learning experience. Plan to attend a couple good ones each year. Don't become a conference "junkie," but learn to use them. They can be absolutely invaluable in terms of making contacts that may result in sales.

But just remember that you have to have that winning manuscript first!

TRENDS AND MARKET INFORMATION

It's important to know "what's selling" and what's not, and what the current trends may be in publishing. You can't ignore trends entirely. At the moment I'm writing this advice to you, for example, I wouldn't try to write another mainstream "coming-of-age" novel on a bet, although I was very successful with such books years ago. Today, everyone I speak with tells me the category is moribund, at least for now. (Next year? Who knows? Some editor may take a chance on one, it might hit big, and then every editor would be looking to buy the same kind of book.)

In a similar way, if you looked at the best-seller lists thirty years ago, you would have found a preponderance of political novels, all thanks to the huge success of Alan Drury's *Advise and Consent.* Then along came Arthur Hailey with *Hotel, Airport* and similar "inside information" novels, and the market was glutted with imitations. Thanks to Stephen King's great successes, everyone started producing novels that tried to be like his. And then came the era of the international thriller, followed by the so-called "techno-thriller" type of best-seller heralded by Tom Clancy.

At this writing, most of those trends are gone, except as exemplified in the continuing works of the big-name novelists who established them in the first place. In the paperbacks, romance novels, a healthy staple for a generation now, are fading somewhat, according to editors I've spoken with. The detective/mystery novel appears healthy, but authors who used to write midlist mainstream novels have been squeezed out by the death of that part of the publishing business, and are scrambling into mystery categories for professional survival, threatening a glut there.

All this simply means that you shouldn't spend all your time trying to outguess the next trend. Far too many writers do far too much of that. The worrying cuts into their production time, for one thing, and trends tend to change fast: If you chase a certain trend right now, and end up writing a really good novel to fit it, you're likely to find out that your manuscript went in six months after the trend died out.

Your job is to be realistic and to stay in touch with the markets, but to spend most of your energy working to perfect your craft. As you grow and analyze others' work, you'll almost automatically find yourself growing in market knowledge and—I hope—making notes in your work journal. This information may be quite enough for you.

Your best sources of market information may be your local bookstore and your librarian. Browse the shelves at the store. Notice what kinds of categories seem to predominate; study several such novels; ask yourself if you could write one like that. Talk to your librarian; ask her what novels have the longest waiting list to be checked out.

Notice the best-seller lists, too. But remember that best-sellers may not represent an attainable trend so much as they might be quirks, one-shots, luck or the result of enormous advertising.

As you study in these ways, your market knowledge will improve. But—again—your first job is improving your product. You can go too far in trying to learn the markets, taking too much time from your development of craftsmanship. I once encountered a would-be novelist who had a big basement office full of filing cabinets stuffed with market information and trend analyses. He knew *everything* about selling the product. Problem: He never learned enough writing technique to be able to produce a decent product.

So, go to the sources I've mentioned, or others you may uncover for yourself, and stay loosely up to date on what's going on where. But remember that trends and tricks of salesmanship are not your first obligation. Your first obligation is to be one hell of a fine writer. Later, whether or not you find an agent, and however you contact the right editor, you can and *will* sell your novel—if it's good enough and isn't totally out of step with everything that's being sold by other writers.

This, too, is all part of the professional attitude we started talking about many pages ago. When I said that the professional learns to "trust the process," I didn't mean that she simply uses good technique, trusting that a good novel will result. I also meant that she trusts that the process of writing a good novel can and will result finally in commercial success.

ASSIGNMENT

Although you've been warned not to get too preoccupied with sales techniques at the expense of writing technique, it's not too early for you to take the first baby steps on learning more about the markets.

Make some notes in your journal about what genre of novel you would like to write next; who your favorite authors are in that genre; what some of the characteristics of that genre seem to be; what some of the things are you may still need to know in terms of (1) getting to know the genre intimately, and (2) learning additional specialized techniques that seem to be favored therein; who the major publishers appear to be at the present time; where you might find an author or editor in that genre appearing at a conference you could attend, and any other activities you should be undertaking to increase your knowledge in the area.

Study and mark up more books of the type you have selected.

If you have not identified a genre, try to generally categorize the kind of book you're working on or hope to start next. How long is it? How large a cast? How lengthy a present-story time span? Is there violence? How much introspection (sequel) *versus* action (scene)? How could you characterize the language generally used—plain and simple, or more ornate, for example?

Make up more questions of your own, and get your journal expanding into these areas right away.

Chapter Nineteen

Final Words

Professional writers write.

Everyone else talks about it.

To succeed, you must be professional; you must stop talking and start doing. In this book I've done my best to show you how a professional goes about the "doing." So now it's up to you. I've known few would-be writers who failed. I've known many who quit.

Here's hoping you won't quit. It has been said that the greatest thing in life is to have a goal and to be working diligently toward it. The world is full of people who make excuses for their failures to try. Don't become one of them. Remember that wanting to write a good novel, and find readers for it, is a noble goal. Once you eschew excuses and steadfastly refuse to allow bitterness, you are embarked on a journey that will enrich your life.

These are tough times in the novel-publishing business. A few known writers are being paid obscene amounts on the basis of their name alone, and legions of lesser lights have been temporarily extinguished. In this atmosphere it's very hard to break in.

However, the fact that things are hard today does not mean they're impossible. The period around 1957–1960 was a bad time in publishing too. I've been told that *no one* broke in then. Luckily, I didn't know it at the time. I heard it only years later, long after I sold my first novel in 1957—and six more in the next two years. So my own experience contradicts the naysayers. It also proves that if you do your work, you too can beat all the odds.

As you move on in your career, take time out now and then

to look back on some of the ideas you've noted in your work journal after studying here. Remember the time-tested techniques, and continue to apply them to your own work.

Dream your story dreams and plan each book carefully.

Write your first draft straight through, without undue second-guessing or wasteful rewriting until that draft is done. Produce pages! Plan to fix them later.

Never give up.

Remember that good novels are are not written, but rewritten.

Trust the process; you *will* get better if you use proven techniques.

Be healthily self-critical: fight to improve, but don't get down on yourself.

Never give up.

Be honest with yourself about the kind of books you like to read and the kind you want to write.

Work to better understand your own feelings; observe people around you in order to understand them better, too.

Make analysis of your own and others' published work an ongoing part of your dedication.

Never give up.

Force yourself to maintain your work journal, and make positive conclusions an integral part of it.

Work hard, and to a disciplined schedule. But take time out to be good to yourself—to your body as well as to your mind.

Never give up.

If you write a good enough book, it *will* sell. And if this one isn't good enough, if you keep analyzing and working and growing and writing, the next one—or the one after that—will be good enough.

And that one will sell.

We have to believe that, all of us. We're in an international competition, you and I, and only the best will survive. But remember this, always: *We can never be beaten unless we give up.*

Let us, then, work to become the best that we can be, and have faith that everything else we dream about will follow.

Good luck!

THE BEGINNING

BIBLIOGRAPHY

Bellow, Saul. *Herzog.* New York: Viking Press, 1964.

Berne, Eric. *Games People Play.* New York: Grove Press, 1964.

Bickham, Jack M. *Katie, Kelly and Heck.* New York: Doubleday, 1973.

Bickham, Jack M. *Scene and Structure.* Cincinnati: Writer's Digest Books, 1993.

Bickham, Jack M. *Setting.* Cincinnati: Writer's Digest Books, 1994.

Campbell, Walter S. *Writing: Advice and Devices.* New York: Doubleday, 1950.

Clinton, Jeff. *The Fighting Buckaroo.* New York: Berkley Medallion, 1961.

Dickens, Charles. *Great Expectations.* Many editions available.

Edmonds, J.M., Ed. *The Characters of Theophrastus.* Cambridge: Harvard University Press, 1946.

Fast, Julius. *Body Language.* New York: Pocket Books, 1971.

Fleming, Ian. *Goldfinger.* New York: Macmillan Co., 1959.

Foster-Harris, William. *The Basic Formulas of Fiction.* Norman: University of Oklahoma Press, 1944.

Grisham, John. *The Rainmaker.* New York: Doubleday, 1995.

Hayakawa, S.I. *Symbol, Status and Personality.* New York: Harcourt, Brace & World, 1963.

Herrigel, Eugen. *Zen in the Art of Archery.* New York: Vintage Books, 1989.

Higgins, Jac. *The Eagle Has Landed.* New York: Bantam Books, 1976.

Hills, Rust. "Fiction," *Esquire*, October, 1973.

Hoffer, Eric. *The Ordeal of Change.* New York: Harper Colophon, 1964. Karpman, S. "Fairy Tales and Script Drama

Analysis." *Transactional Analysis Bulletin*, 1968.

Leonard, Elmore. *Rum Punch*. New York: Delacorte Press, 1992.

MacDonald, John D. *Darker Than Amber*. New York: Gold Medal, 1966.

Steere, David A. *Bodily Expressions in Psychotherapy*. New York: Brunner/Mazel, 1982.

Steiner, Claude M. *Scripts People Live*. New York: Grove Press, 1974.

Swain, Dwight V. *Tricks and Techniques of the Selling Writer*. Norman: University of Oklahoma Press, 1965.

Thrall, William Flint, and Addison Hibbard. *A Handbook to Literature*. New York: Odyssey Press, 1960.

Wellek, Rene, and Austin Warren. *Theory of Literature*. New York: Harcourt, Brace, 1949.

Whitney, Phyllis A. *The Trembling Hills*. New York: Fawcett Crest, 1965.

Wouk, Herman. *The Caine Mutiny*. New York: Doubleday, 1951.

INDEX

A

Agents, 199, 202-203
Ambition, 11-12
Answer, to story question, 74-75
Antagonist, role of, in motivation, 73-74
Attribution, use of, 163-164

B

Background, vs. stimulus, 67-69
Backstory, 175-178
  temptations of, 178-179
Beginning, with change, 84-85
Best-seller. *See* Fiction, popular
Body language, 168

C

Change
  acceptance of, 7, 15-16
  importance of, 83-84
  in manuscript, 22
  starting with, 84-85
Character
  building up, 131
  history of, 133-134
  intentionally dishonest, 148-149
  introducing, 86-87, 138-143
  name of, 131-132
  necessary exaggeration of, 29-30
  uniqueness of, through viewpoint, 56-57
  vs. concept, 77-78
  See also Self-concept, Viewpoint character
Characteristic entry action, defined, 139-140
Characteristic preoccupation, 144-145
Characterization
  errors in, 195
  through internalization, 67
Clarity, in dialogue, 167
Climax
  delaying, with obstacles, 76-78
  See also Goal

Comment by other characters, defined, 139, 141-142
Computer, writing on, 19
Conflict
  character-testing, 29-32
  errors in, 195
  as major element, 96-97
  vs. adversity, 31
  See also Change
Criticism, of manuscript, seeking, 198-199
Crossed transaction, 155-156
Culture, and setting, 118

D

Denial, 150-151
Description, 37, 125-126
  setting, 113-115
Dialogue, 124-125, 168-169
  components of, 163
  in and out of scene, 162-163
  role-playing for, 192
Dialogue fragments, 170
Direct author intrusion, defined, 139, 142-143
Disaster, scenic, nature of, 97-100
Displacement behavior, 152-153
Drama Triangle, 157-158
Dramatic action, 124
Dramatic summary, 123-124

E

Editing. *See* Revision
Editors, 199
Ending, 87-92
Exercises
  backstory and hidden story, 181-182
  beginnings and endings, 92
  character, 145-146
  dialogue and narration, 172
  genre identification, 207
  goal analysis, 82
  outline, 191-192

revision, 200
setting analysis, 119
stimulus and response, 72
story time, 126-127
viewpoint analysis, 55-56
writing viewpoint, 57-60
Exposition, 126

F

Fiction, popular, 10
as current model, 14-15
Flashback. *See* Backstory, temptations of
Foster-Harris, William, 28, 88-89

G

Genre novel, as learning ground, 201-202
Goal, 74-80
clarity of, 96
defining character through, 134

H

Hidden story, 175, 179-181
Hills, Rust, 48

I

Imagination, aids to, 22-24
Internalization, 65-67, 165-166
Introduction by habitat, defined, 139, 141

L

Leonard, Elmore, 53-54
Life Script, 158-159
Logic, errors in, 195

M

Manuscript, representing own, 202-203
Motivation
background, vs. stimulus, 67-69
positive, values of, 73-74
and self-concept, 80-82
See also Goal

N

Narration, 125
principles of, 169
Neutral passages, handling, 52-54
Novel. *See* Story

O

Obstacles, 10-11, 76-78
Omniscience, 46-47
Opening. *See* Beginning

P

Pace, controlling, 105, 121-126, 195
Paragraphs, separate, for stimulus and response, 71
Personality, exaggeration of, 129-131
Plot, starting with, vs. character, 80-81
Plot review, 170
Projection, 149-150
Psychology, character's
impact of, on goal selection, 78-80
See also Crossed transaction; Denial; Displacement behavior; Life Script; Projection; Reaction, character's; Transactional Analysis
Publishing, trends in, 204-206
Purple prose, avoiding, 38

Q

Query letters, to agents, 202-203
Quota, production, 5, 20

R

Reaction, character's, 151-152
Reader, intentionally puzzling, 67
Reader orientation, 38-39, 195
Research, 8
Response, tailoring, 69-70
See also Stimulus and response
Revision, 196-198

S

Scene
dialogue in and out of, 162-163
nature of, 94
structure of, 95-96

Scene openers, 38-40
Scene-sequel, plot demands and
    manipulations of, 183-187
Scene, or sequel
    distinguishing, from incident,
    104-105
    interruption of, 187
    skipping, 187-188
Schulberg, Budd, 49
Self-concept, 134-136
    and change, 83-84
    and goal selection, 79-82
Sequel
    segments of, 102-104
    structure of, 100-102
Sequel thought, 170
Setting
    factual information about, 115-116
    key points on, 118-119
    knowledge of, 112-113
    selection of, 111-112
Setting description, 170-171
Stage action, 38-40, 164-165
Stimuli, avoiding too many, 70-71
Stimulus, vs. background motivation,
    67-69
Stimulus and response, 61-66
Story
    as formed record, 28
    as movement, 32-35
    good, features of, 28
Story question, 75-76
Structure
    controlling pace through, 121-123
    of scene, 95-96
    of sequel, 100-102
    viewpoint-change tactics relating

    to, 189-190
Swain, Dwight V., 93

T

Tags, 136-138
Talent, and professionalism, 3
Techniques of the Selling Writer, 93
Time setting, 117-118, 195
    See also Pace, controlling
Traits, 136-138
Transactional Analysis, 153-155

V

Viewpoint
    changing, 188-190
    establishing, 49-50
    reinforcement of, 50-51
    restriction of, 45-46
    "temperature" of, 54-55
    use of, 32
    within scene, 108
Viewpoint character
    and goal motivation, 73-74
    selection of, 46-49
Viewpoint observations, restricting,
    51-52
Vignette, 33-34

W

Whitney, Phyllis A., 186
Writer's conferences, 203-204
Writer's Market, 202
Writing
    on computer, 19
    dedication to, 5-6
    process of, trusting in, 8-9
    setting quota for, 5

More Great Books for Writers!

1997 Writer's Market: Where & How to Sell What You Write—Get your work into the right buyers' hands and save yourself the frustration of getting manuscripts returned in the mail. You'll find 4,000 listings loaded with submission information, as well as real life interviews on scriptwriting, networking, freelancing and more! *#10457/$27.99/1008 pages*

Now Available on CD-ROM!

1997 Writer's Market Electronic Edition—Customize your marketing research and speed to the listings that fit your needs using this compact, searchable CD-ROM! *#10492/$39.99*

1997 Writer's Market Combination Package—For maximum usability, order both the book and CD-ROM in one convenient package! *#45148/$49.99*

Get That Novel Written: From Initial Idea to Final Edit—Take your novel from the starting line to a fabulous finish! Professional writer Donna Levin shows you both the basics and the finer points of novel writing while you learn to use words with precision, create juicy conflicts, master point of view and more! *#10481/$18.99/208 pages*

The Writer's Essential Desk Reference—Get quick, complete, accurate answers to your important writing questions with this companion volume to *Writer's Market*. You'll cover all aspects of the business side of writing—from information on the World Wide Web and other research sites to opportunities with writers' workshops and the basics on taxes and health insurance. *#10485/$24.99/384 pages*

Amateur Detectives: A Writer's Guide to How Private Citizens Solve Criminal Cases—Make your amateur-crime-solver novels and stories accurate and convincing! You'll investigate what jobs work well with sleuthing, information-gathering methods, the law as it relates to amateur investigators and more! *#10487/$16.99/240 pages/paperback*

The Writer's Digest Dictionary of Concise Writing—Make your work leaner, crisper and clearer! Under the guidance of professional editor Robert Hartwell Fiske, you'll learn how to rid your work of common say-nothing phrases while making it tighter and easier to read and understand. *#10482/$19.99/352 pages*

The Writer's Guide to Everyday Life in Renaissance England—Give your readers a new view of Renaissance England, brimming with the details of daily life. With this one-of-a-kind reference you'll discover a world of facts—from fashions and courtship, to life in the Royal Court and religious festivals. *#10484/$18.99/272 pages/20 b&w illus.*

How to Write Attention-Grabbing Query & Cover Letters—Use the secrets Wood reveals to write queries perfectly tailored, too good to turn down! In this guidebook, you will discover why boldness beats blandness in queries every time, ten basics you *must* have in your article queries, ten query blunders that can destroy publication chances and much more. *#10462/ $17.99/208 pages*

Writing the Blockbuster Novel—Let a top-flight agent show you how to weave the essential elements of a blockbuster into your own novels with memorable characters, exotic settings, clashing conflicts and more! *#10393/$18.99/224 pages*

Get That Novel Started! (And Keep It Going 'Til You Finish)—If you're ready for a no excuses approach to starting and completing your novel, then you're ready for this get-it-going game plan. You'll discover wisdom, experience and advice that helps you latch on to an idea and see it through while avoiding common writing pitfalls. *#10332/$17.99/176 pages*

How to Write a Book Proposal—Don't sabotage your great ideas with a so-so proposal. This guide includes a complete sample proposal, a nine-point Idea Test to check the salability of your book ideas, plus hot tips to make your proposal a success! *#10173/$12.99/136 pages/paperback*

1996 Novel & Short Story Writer's Market—Get the information you need to get your short stories and novels published. You'll discover 1,900 listed fiction publishers in this new edition, plus original articles on fiction writing technique; detailed subject categories to help you target appropriate publishers; and interviews with writers, publishers and editors! *#10441/ $22.99/624 pages/paperback*

Writing to Sell, Fourth Edition—You'll discover high-quality writing and marketing counsel in this classic writing guide from well-known agent Scott Meredith. His timeless advice will guide you along the professional writing path as you get help with creating characters, plotting a novel, placing your work, formatting a manuscript, deciphering a publishing contract—even combating a slump! *#10476/$17.99/240 pages*

Writer's Encyclopedia, Third Edition—Rediscover this popular writer's reference—now with information about electronic resources, plus more than 100 new entries. You'll find facts, figures, definitions and examples designed to answer questions about every discipline connected with writing and help you convey a professional image. *#10464/$22.99/560 pages/62 b&w illus.*

Discovering the Writer Within: 40 Days to More Imaginative Writing—Uncover the creative individual inside who will, with encouragement, turn secret thoughts and special moments into enduring words. You'll learn how to find something exciting in unremarkable places, write punchy first sentences for imaginary stories, give a voice to inanimate objects and much more! *#10472/$14.99/192 pages/paperback*

The Writer's Digest Sourcebook for Building Believable Characters—Create unforgettable characters as you "attend" a roundtable where six novelists reveal their approaches to characterization. You'll probe your characters' backgrounds, beliefs and desires with a fill-in-the-blanks questionnaire. And a thesaurus of characteristics will help you develop the many other features no character should be without. *#10463/$17.99/288 pages*

The Writer's Legal Guide, Revised Edition—Now the answer to all your legal questions is right at your fingertips! The updated version of this treasured desktop companion contains essential information on business issues, copyright protection and registration, contract negotiation, income taxation, electronic rights and much, much more. *#10478/$19.95/256 pages/paperback*

World-Building—Write fiction that transports readers from this world to another . . . of your making. You'll mix elements and build planets with chemically credible and geologically accurate characteristics as you uncover a myriad of topics including facts on gravity, atmospheric science, star types and much more! *#10470/$16.99/224 pages/14 b&w illus.*

Write Tight: How to Keep Your Prose Sharp, Focused and Concise—Discover how to say exactly what you want with grace and power, using the right word and the right number of words. Specific instruction and helpful exercises will help you make your writing compact, concise and precise. *#10360/$16.99/192 pages*

Setting—Expert instruction on using sensual detail, vivid language and keen observation will help you create settings that provide the perfect backdrop to every story. *#10397/$14.99/176 pages*

Conflict, Action & Suspense—Discover how to grab your reader with an action-packed beginning, build the suspense throughout your story and bring it all to a fever pitch through powerful, gripping conflict. *#10396/$14.99/176 pages*
